*f*P

Unveiled

HOW AN AMERICAN WOMAN FOUND
HER WAY THROUGH POLITICS, LOVE, AND
OBEDIENCE IN THE MIDDLE EAST

DEBORAH KANAFANI

Free Press

New York   London   Toronto   Sydney

FREE PRESS
A Division of Simon & Schuster, Inc.
1230 Avenue of the Americas
New York, NY 10020

First Free Press hardcover edition January 2008

FREE PRESS and colophon are trademarks of Simon & Schuster, Inc.

For information about special discounts for bulk purchases,
please contact Simon & Schuster Special Sales at
1-800-456-6798 or business@simonandschuster.com

Designed by Kyoko Watanabe

Manufactured in the United States of America

10   9   8   7   6   5   4   3   2   1

Library of Congress Cataloging-in-Publication Data
Kanafani, Deborah.
Unveiled / Deborah Kanafani.
1. Kanafani, Deborah. 2. Women—Middle East—Biography.
3. Women's rights—Middle East. I. Title.
HQ1726.5.Z75K35 2007
306.89'3092—dc22
2007020699
ISBN-13: 978-0-7432-9183-5
ISBN-10: 0-7432-9183-2

To the two loves of my life, Deena and Tarik,
and for my father, whose colorful life left us
with more stories than we could tell in a lifetime.

CONTENTS

CONTENTS

Author's Note

While living in Ramallah, Palestine, from 1997 to 2000, I was introduced to Jim Marrioni, the playwright-in-residence at New York University. He had been sent to the area by the U.S. State Department's people-to-people outreach program, tasked with starting the first Jordanian-Israeli-Palestinian theater group in an effort to nurture reconciliation. His program was highly successful. The actors were able to work through their emotions on stage and even developed a bond as they realized how similar their lives truly were. Marrioni decided to write a play for them: the story of a group of actors who tire of performing the same scenes night after night. They complain to their director and ask for a new ending. The old director, comfortable with his familiar ending, resists. The play examines change, resistance, and the need for new endings—a powerful metaphor for the repetitious scenes we play out day after day, year after year, in our own lives

This book is about people who try to find new endings, from the large-scale arena of global politics to a woman's freedom within her own household. Each woman who comes forward in this book is trying to give her life a new ending. I too was determined to create a new ending to a predictable scenario, one in which I felt dominated and marginalized. My challenge was to create a happy, safe ending for my children and never lose sight of that goal. I lost custody of my two children in the Middle East and uprooted my life, from the United States to Palestine, to be with them. The route wasn't always easy, but on my way, I encountered many inspirational women who served as guides. This book also examines some of the interpretations of Islamic laws and the views of Islamic women wishing to change these interpretations. It is in no way intended to criticize Islam; in fact, the women embrace their religion and often state that the laws imposed on them do not reflect the true essence of Islamic religious teachings.

I believe that peace can prevail between Palestinians and Israelis. I do not see one side as right and the other as wrong. There are people on both sides who want peace. I was in the Middle East when Israelis and Palestinians were openly reaching out to one another. These peacemakers still exist, and they expand their circles every day, although they are not seen on the news. I hope you will see this hidden side and support these people, Israelis and Palestinians, who are taking peace into their own hands.

Unveiled

CHAPTER ONE

Some Memories

MY IMAGINATION IS A GIFT FROM MY MATERNAL GREAT-grandmother, Fahimi Kirban. She had come to America from Lebanon many years before I was born and lived in a house across the street from my parents on New York's Long Island. When I was growing up in the late 1950s, I spent countless hours with her. There were many things that fascinated me about my great-grandmother, but most of all, I was intrigued by the tattoos traced on her arms by the wandering gypsies of her homeland when she was a little girl. Barely old enough to cross the street, I would run to her house each morning, jump on a chair at the kitchen table, and beg her to tell me the same gypsy tales over and over again.

She grew up in a small Lebanese village nestled above the Mediterranean that had been inhabited by sea-trading Phoenicians and, later, the Romans. The Lebanese were said to be descendants of the Phoenicians, giving them an inherent love of travel and trading. Fahimi's father was a simple man who grew fruits and vegetables on his land. He was as solid as the earth under his feet, strong in a quiet way—unlike her opinionated mother, who did most of the talking for both of them.

Her mother had been assigned to her father in an arranged marriage and, like Fahimi, had been cursed (or blessed) with the restless Phoenician spirit. She was a sturdy, capable woman who would have done well working the land if she had so desired. Instead, she spent her days listening to stories of people who had left for America from those who'd remained. She shortened her name from Anastasia to the more American-sounding "Annie," making it easier to imagine herself in the land she longed to visit, so far away.

Fahimi shared her mother's imagination, and her mind often wandered while she did her daily chores. She took her pet donkey to the nearby springs each morning and gathered water in old clay pots. She then passed by the family orchards to gather the ripened apples and sweet pomegranates, placing them in her donkey's harness. On occasion, while picking fruit, she heard the music of the gypsies. She knew the people in her village despised them: they were rumored to steal fruit, and the villagers feared that one day, they would even steal their children. But Fahimi was entranced by the sounds of their handmade instruments, and instead of walking home, she often changed direction and wandered up the hills to watch the forbidden gypsies. She loved the sight of their fabrics, painted in fuchsia and gold, that hung over their shoulders. When they saw their shy little visitor approaching, they greeted her, eyeing the fruits that she was supposed to carry home.

Fahimi was fascinated by the gypsies' hands, both young and old, decorated with tattoos of serpents and flowers, stars and half-moons. She silently watched them reach into her baskets. They held the shiny apples while looking at her, indicating that they would trade the fruit for her very own tattoos. After a few intense, silent moments, she would nod in agreement. And so they put pots on the fire to boil the color out of berries and barks, creating a palette. The band gathered around as the elder gypsy women told tales while inscribing exotic flowers in strangely shaped vases on her inner arms. When they finished, they took turns admiring their work. As she got closer to home (and to the spanking she knew would come), their music faded, but not the memories. Years later, when Fahimi's father was caught courting another woman, Annie packed up Fahimi and her siblings and set out for America—but not before taking a trip up the hills with Fahimi and getting two small roosters tattooed on her own chest. Eventually she became a successful entrepreneur in America, selling linens and fabrics from all over the world: she bought one of the first cars and hired a chauffeur to drive her from house to house to see her customers. She sold everything for a nickel, and thus her name became Annie Nickels. I wanted to be like Annie and Fahimi when I grew up.

I studied Fahimi every day: I watched her walk in her gardens, tending to her Japanese lace maples, her grape vines, and her roses as she kept a close eye on the bulbs she had planted, waiting for them to bloom in the spring. Many people came to see her roses—she even won awards for them—but I always liked the bulbs, living quietly in the darkness until they were ready to bloom. I felt like them, safely hidden just under the surface, blossoming only under her watchful eye. Fahimi had six daughters in addition to my grandmother and no sons. They were strong, tough women, confident and grand. I was wrapped in a cocoon of feminine energy. They all argued a lot, because they were opinionated, but they always left with warm hugs and kisses. No one argued with Fahimi. She was the matriarch, and she was my closest friend.

In the evenings we went to the untouched bedroom of her youngest daughter, Naomi, who had died in childbirth before I was born. We sat in the dark and looked out the window at Fahimi's favorite weeping willow tree as it swayed in the wind. Naomi and her child died at the same moment. For a short period of time, she was laid out in this bedroom, wearing her wedding dress, with her baby in her arms. At night her husband came to the room and rocked his lifeless baby in a rocking chair. They say he went crazy and was never seen again after the burial. As I sat on her lap, not letting on that I was looking at Naomi's picture more than I was looking at the weeping willow tree, I couldn't help thinking that I looked like Naomi, and I wondered if Fahimi thought the same. She rubbed my back with her calloused hands, rough from her work in the garden, and I felt a strange safety despite my eerie surroundings. My time with her was serene and charmed, unlike the discord in my parents' home.

My parents met when my father was finishing law school. He didn't have a large family like my mother; in fact, he knew only his mother. His mother and father had left Lebanon when she was pregnant with him and went to Mexico, where he was born. From there, his parents decided to come to the United States separately because it was easier for a woman alone with a child to gain entry. She settled in the Lebanese community in Brooklyn when he was seven. They never saw my grandfather again. Many years later they found out that he had been killed in a brawl while crossing the Mexican border.

My grandmother and father stayed with nuns she had known from her village, and she worked in a factory. They struggled financially during his childhood, and so my father yearned for a bigger life; he was ambitious, with huge dreams. Mutual family friends had invited him and his mother to my great-grandmother Fahimi's home for a party. He was twenty-eight at the time, and my mother was eighteen. Used to living in Brooklyn, my father kept commenting that my great-grandmother's gardens made him feel as if he was in Hawaii. Evidently that day, he charmed three generations of women, from my mother to my great-grandmother. My mother married him a few months later. I was born the next year, and my brother, Mark, followed just thirteen months later. It was the late 1950s, and my mother, a typical housewife of the era, was happy with her life, and she didn't share my father's glamorous ambitions. After my father established his law practice, he moved us a few blocks away into an imposing house that sat on top of a hill. It was constructed with large stones and had a porch in the back overlooking the woods. I know there must have been lights in my parents' house, but I remember it only as dark.

Their marriage ended abruptly one evening shortly after we moved. I was six years old. I always waited for my father to come home, and as soon as he opened the front door, I would run to him fast enough to feel as if I was flying. He always managed to grab me at just the right moment, lifting me up as high as he could, helping me take flight. He had that kind of power to me: he could make me feel that anything was possible. I didn't know my mother was waiting for him on this particular evening. She had found evidence of an adulterous affair, so when he arrived, they exchanged angry words. I didn't understand; I knew only that something frightening was happening. I panicked as he grabbed some clothes and headed toward the door. My mother and I were both crying, and she ran to her room. I ran to the door, calling him, but he couldn't hear me. I saw his car's taillights vanish in the distance, and I felt a void so deep that all I could do was scream.

He was gone for only a few days before visiting my brother and me, but those few days felt like an eternity. My mother packed up our belongings, and we moved to a small house in another town. My maternal grandfather came to stay with us and help her. She was young and had no way to support us, aside from the little help she received from my father. He often picked us up in his big convertible Cadillac and took us to the park. He acted as if it was a coincidence that he always ran into the same beautiful woman with teased red hair each time we strolled by the duck pond. My mother remained angry at him for breaking up the family and having her dreams shattered.

Within a year, my father married the woman he used to meet in the park, and my mother married a handsome former Marine who was devoted to the family life she craved. She cut my father out of all the family pictures and tried to make believe that he didn't exist. We moved to Long Island, into a neighborhood called Island Trees mostly composed of World War II veterans. Our closely knit neighborhood was home to solid people with old-fashioned values, who became our extended family. Our neighbors were our "aunts and uncles." There were no luxuries. Our life was simple and full of routines. My mother liked to cook an early family dinner, and afterward the neighborhood kids would gather in our yard to play. It was a stable and predictable life, worlds away from the decadent life my father was living in a nearby town.

My parents spent a great deal of time battling for custody and disagreed about every detail of our upbringing, my mother wanting us to be in her world and my father in his. Half the week, I lived in my mother's world. I spent the other half in my father's domain, in one of the most spectacular homes in Kings Point on the Long Island Sound—the land of extravagance that so inspired F. Scott Fitzgerald in the 1920s. We had a full staff, including a chauffeur who drove me to my friends' house. When my father first drove me to the home in Kings Point, he looked at me in the rearview mirror and said, "Kid, I'm taking you to the stars."

I was torn between two people who had an undying dislike for each other, and I never really felt that I belonged in either place. To say I lived at one parent's house meant that the other parent would be angry. My real home became internal, a place inside me, protected. My parents' battles continued for years, and I was caught in the cross fire, trying to figure out how to keep both parents happy. I sat through several courtroom custody battles as my parents stared at me and the judge demanded to know with whom I wanted to live. Inevitably someone would end up hurt. When we weren't in court, I was playing the mediator in this chronic state of war.

I was certain about one thing: my father adored me. He had three more sons with my stepmother, and I was his only daughter. They dressed me up and took me out to the finest restaurants in New York City and to plays and ballets. He was a charismatic man who charmed everyone and made us laugh all the time. He held huge parties at his home, and his childhood friends from Brooklyn came with their children. Everyone stayed for the weekend, listening to the music of Frank Sinatra or being entertained by hired belly dancers. It was a nonstop whirlwind of fun. At the hub was the hero of it all, my father. To him, this was life: having enough wealth to be in the spotlight, the world revolving around him. My father not only loved to be the center of attention, he needed to be. And he was good at it. He told stories about fantastic trials and hour-long summations that had persuaded his juries. On occasion, I went to court and watched his trials. I was intimidated by his ability to destroy someone on the witness stand and shoot me a smile just moments later.

When he wasn't entertaining at home, he was planning exciting vacations. I remember bringing a friend on a trip to the

Bahamas when I was twelve. While we were out on a private diving boat with several instructors, my father dropped his small cigarette holder overboard—and then hired divers to find it. The next day he didn't like the lounge chairs by the pool, so he had special chairs flown in from our house on Long Island. When we returned home, my friend told everyone at school what happened. This was the first time I realized how unusual his behavior was.

I went to live with my father and stepmother when I entered high school. My father had convinced my mother that it was best for me to attend a private high school near his house. He had always wanted to oversee my education. On the weekends he sent me to New York University for additional courses in art history and literature because he wanted me to be knowledgeable about current events and culture. As he told me, he wanted me to be an intelligent wife and a good conversationalist at a dinner party. He hadn't considered that I could have a life and use my education for purposes beyond complementing the professional aspirations of a suitable husband.

He used his own education in the law to figure out how to get around it. He wanted to make his own rules. He told my brothers and me not to bother getting driver's licenses and urged us to park in illegal spots. One day I saw yellow paint in his trunk, and when I asked about it, he told me that the curb outside his favorite restaurant was painted red, indicating that parking wasn't allowed. He decided to paint it yellow in the middle of the night so he could park there. He didn't want us to save money or do anything that would give us any independence. He expected us to support anything he did. If talk of my brothers' future came up, the idea that any of them might not work for him was unthinkable. He wanted us dependent on him—or in trouble so he could save us.

Toward the end of my high school years in the 1970s, he began to take his career in a new direction. It started when a man who had been accused of theft wanted my father to defend him. The man had been working at a car dealership, selling nonexistent warranties to car buyers. My father thought this concept was brilliant, and so he adapted the idea but did it legitimately. He contacted auto manufacturers and invited them to his offices to tell them all about "his" new extended warranty program. To prepare for the meetings, he arranged for the other tenants in the building to allow him to break through the walls between their offices and his. This way, it appeared that all the offices were part of his company. He hired actors to fill the desks, and he had my brothers and me hard at work in the downstairs lobby, calling the "offices" over and over again so the phones were ringing.

The auto manufacturers loved it and signed on for his programs. He was building an empire overnight. It would come to be called Republic Warranty, which thousands of car dealerships used and ultimately gave him the empire he sought. He soon had more than 500 employees, and with this success came more grandiose behavior. He loved having so many people to control. I attended one large meeting of new executives without letting on I was his daughter. At one point, when he left the room, they began telling one another that the first names they had used to introduce themselves during the meeting weren't their actual names. They all said my father had told them there were too many people with their name in the company, and he assigned a new name for them to use. The men were perplexed, but I knew my father had done this just for the pure enjoyment of knowing that he could.

Meanwhile, I took an apartment in Manhattan and enrolled at the New School for Social Research. I was studying psychology and obtained an internship that allowed me to help start the first shelter for battered women in New York City. I helped the women and their children get settled in apartments the shelter provided for them at the Henry Street Settlement in Lower Manhattan. I enjoyed the time I spent with these families more than I enjoyed the world of superficial people who surrounded my father. When I was honored at my school at a luncheon with 200 people, my mother and stepfather, always supportive, attended. My father, as usual, was too busy and made no effort to come. I knew he adored me and would light up when I walked in the room, but I craved something more from this elusive man.

My father relocated to California with my stepmother and their three young sons while I was still in college, moving into one of the fabulous Rat Pack houses in Palm Springs. I stayed in New York to study. In addition to my class work, I attended the Gestalt Institute and the Rational Emotive Institute and explored new theories of humanistic psychology. I was trying to make sense of my bizarre upbringing, I suppose. My father continued his decadent lifestyle in California until he was again caught having an affair, and my stepmother and he divorced. He began traveling more to New York and often took my friends and me out for dinner and to private nightclubs. My friends adored him and all his charisma. There were few other people who were as much fun or as entertaining as he was, and I had become so used to his grand gestures that other men's lives seemed mundane. That is, until I met the prince.

CHAPTER TWO

The Prince

LEANING OVER THE RAIL OF THE *QUEEN ELIZABETH II*, on a sunny spring afternoon in 1980, I waved farewell to my family and watched as their silhouettes dissolved into the New York City skyline. I was a graduate student, taking my first trip to Europe, where I'd arranged to meet friends at the Cannes Film Festival. Crossing the Atlantic to France, where I would disembark, would take five days; then the ship would go on to England. I had chosen the *QE2* because of its reputation—the formal vessel with Old World charm had such romantic appeal to me. I imagined wind in my hair, water rushing past. I was exhilarated by the thought of the ship's energy. While gazing at the diminishing city, I heard the announcement that high tea would be served at 4:00 P.M. I left the deck and wandered into the tearoom, content to sit alone and reflect on the journey ahead.

As I sipped my tea, I noticed a beautifully dressed woman glide through the room as if she owned it. She seated herself at the table next to mine and placed her order, her words colored by an unfamiliar accent. She glanced at me, half-smiling, then turned and introduced herself. She explained that she was the wife of a Jordanian general. She, her husband, and ten others were accompanying a prince from their country on the transatlantic trip. Her words rung in my ears. Before I boarded the ship, I'd laughingly declared to my family that I planned to meet a prince on the voyage. Of course, they had dismissed my statement.

As we spoke, a group of men appeared at the tearoom entrance and gestured for her to join them. She looked up for a moment at a well-dressed man waving impatiently at her. Then she turned to me as if she didn't recognize him. "My husband," she said. "Don't ever go when a man calls. Wait for him to come to you." We continued our conversation and eventually the gentlemen approached the table. They were polite and friendly, and when they learned I was traveling alone, they insisted I join them for dinner that evening.

I was reluctant to accept the invitation. The ship was strictly class segregated, and although I was traveling very comfortably, my appointed dining room was not designated for royalty. I feared the maître d' might not even allow me entrance to their quarters. Nevertheless, their kind persistence convinced me to join them. Sure enough, at 7:00 P.M. sharp, there was a knock at my cabin door. One of the royal guards traveling with the entourage announced that he was to escort me to the dining room. I didn't know if the prince would be present at dinner. When I arrived, the host greeted me by name, then led me to the table. Obviously he'd been briefed on my arrival. Any apprehension I had quickly melted away. The dining room was breathtaking; its walls were draped in rich, red velvet, with windows on both sides that opened to endless miles of ocean. A fiery sunset filled the sky. Guests were dressed in formal attire—men in tuxedos and women in evening gowns; the dining staff wore white gloves and crisp uniforms.

The mood at the table was festive. When I mentioned that my family was from Lebanon, the prince's entourage became excited and swore to protect and take care of me for the rest of the journey. It felt as if I was being initiated into some sort of bedouin tribe. With each Arabic phrase I uttered, remembering bits and pieces from childhood, their acceptance of me grew.

Suddenly guests stopped their chatter and rose from their seats. Two Jordanian men in starched military uniforms entered the room. Behind them came the prince, followed by two more uniformed men. As the prince circled the table, his escorts saluted while the others remained at attention. Eventually he positioned himself behind the vacant chair next to me. He was a handsome man with fine features; I recalled my new friend mentioning that he was ten years older than me and recently divorced. The prince and I shyly smiled at each other, and he gestured for me to sit down. Then he sat, thereby signaling the rest of the guests to do the same.

The general and his wife sat across from me. It was the general's responsibility to make all formal introductions. One of my tablemates whispered to me that the prince was always to be addressed as "Your Highness." The next few moments were slightly awkward as the prince and I tried to look at each other without being too obvious. Finally I broke the ice. Shifting in his direction, I told him that I was on my way to the Cannes Film Festival. Adopting a casual tone, I inquired about his interest in cinema, expecting to hear names of celebrated French or Italian directors like Truffaut or Bertolucci. Instead, he told me that his favorite film was *Jaws* and that he was a huge fan of John Wayne westerns.

I was amused by his simplicity. Our dinner conversation was light and, I quickly assessed, was solely for his entertainment. My dinner companions asked me to repeat all the Arabic phrases I knew, and he laughed with delight. When our food arrived, the general informed me from across the table that no one was to eat until the prince surveyed each person's meal. If anyone's dinner looked more appetizing, he reserved the right to exchange his meal for theirs. I asked what would happen if I decided I might like to have the prince's meal instead of mine. My challenge was met with dead silence, broken only by the prince's laughter. Relieved, everyone joined in, and they told me they had been teasing me amiably and were amused by my response. I knew my father, the rule breaker, would be proud of me.

The rest of the dinner went smoothly, and I was invited to have lunch with the group the next day and then take a tour of the ship. I insisted that we see a film in the afternoon, choose some books from the library, and take a walk around the deck. His entourage stayed a few steps behind, careful not to interfere with my agenda, since the prince seemed to be enjoying himself.

That evening, the ship's captain hosted a predinner cocktail party for the prince and other distinguished guests. The prince asked that I attend with him, so once again his guards were sent to escort me to the party. People addressed me as "Your Highness," assuming I was royalty too. The prince didn't correct them, and I certainly didn't. I was enjoying the charade. After being escorted back to my cabin at the end of a long evening, I decided to take a walk and socialize with other people on the ship. I sat and spoke with a group from New York, but I could see the prince's guards watching me from an outside deck.

There was a similar schedule the following day, highlighted by music and dancing after dinner at one of the ship's nightclubs. We were sitting rather stiffly around a table when the prince slipped out with some of his aides. The general and I danced several times. A few passengers approached and asked me to dance as well, but I declined. Shortly after, one of the prince's aides appeared and asked that we join the prince in his cabin. His quarters were wrapped in marble and boasted an imposing staircase winding to a second floor. We sipped champagne and were led to a table that had been staged for a card game. We played some simple games—nothing that required much attention. Later that evening, the general's wife told me that the aides had reported to the prince that I hadn't danced with any of the other passengers. In their culture, it is considered improper if a woman dances with a strange man. I had passed their test.

I had also quickly become friends with the prince's doctor. He wasn't especially affected by the royal trappings and was a stable presence for me. He noticed the prince's newfound cheer and started hinting that I would make a good wife for him. In the Middle East, decisions like this were often made after one or two meetings. And so our days continued with lunch, tea, trapshooting on the deck, and formal dinners. The group was refreshing for me, playful and devoted to making sure the prince was having a good time. I was enjoying the taste of royal life, with people hovering around to fulfill every need and treating me with impeccable manners.

When we were a day from completing our five-day journey to France, where I planned to disembark, the doctor asked to speak with me alone. He wanted to know if I would be willing to change my plans and continue on to London with them. Although I was looking forward to Cannes, I assented and canceled my plans.

When the ship arrived in Southampton, the general instructed me to wait in my cabin. I could hear announcements being made, informing the passengers how to proceed with immigration at the port. I was concerned about the long lines that I assumed were building up and wanted to leave my room. Then there was a knock at my door. Two immigration officers, sent to stamp my passport, entered. I could see that everything was going to be done differently now.

After disembarking, we were escorted through the port by the British military and a marching band. Jordan had been ruled by Great Britain before gaining its independence in 1943, and the two countries maintained a mutual deference, resulting in ceremonies such as this. A motorcade of classic black Rolls Royces was waiting to take us to London. I challenged myself to act as though I regularly traveled in such a manner. My father always told me to never act impressed by anyone, and I decided to follow his advice. I was driven with the general's wife, while the prince rode in front of us with the Jordanian ambassador to Great Britain. We arrived at the posh Dorchester Hotel, where I was checked in and given a room down the hall from the general and his wife. The prince was taken to his family's royal apartment in St. James's Square.

Our relationship was formal and proper; we were never alone together. I had called my family from the ship and told them about my change in plans. My mother wanted me to contact my stepfather's relatives in London so that someone could make sure that I was being watched over and not taken advantage of. I spoke to my father from time to time and heard from friends that he was telling everyone I was probably going to marry a prince.

A routine was quickly established after our arrival in London. The prince was picked up and driven to the Dorchester at 4:00 every afternoon, where he held court in the tearoom while visitors came to see him. I loved the formality of these gatherings and was amused at how seriously people took them. I felt like an insider and an outsider at the same time. When business associates, family friends, or some British officials arrived, a large section of the tearoom was commandeered. Staff members were on hand to serve the prince and his guests, and his security detail filled several seating areas. I was torn between enjoying the feeling of complete privilege and restlessness, when I remembered that there was another world out there that I wanted to explore, like the wonderful paintings at the Tate.

During these few weeks, I relied on the general's wife, who advised me about protocol when I accompanied the prince on formal visits or dinners. She was the closest I had to a confidante. I was never told more than a few hours in advance what had been scheduled; I was expected to be available and wait until I was given instructions. One day, she told me that the prince wanted to invite me to his apartment and that I should bring a dinner dress with me since we would be picked up from there for the evening. I thought this was unusual, but I was flattered that the prince was inviting me into his personal space. Maybe the formality between us would soften.

It was a beautiful apartment, tastefully furnished in navy and white. The servants' quarters were as large as the living quarters, to accommodate the tremendous staff that accompanied him. He had the television on when I arrived, and I realized quickly that he expected me to sit and watch with him. I was served some refreshments, and then someone came in to inform me of dinner plans and offered to show me to a room where I could change. It was luxurious, with a grand dressing room. I took my time and sat in front of an old French vanity surrounded by mirrors. The maids brought me tea and helped me get dressed. I really did feel like a princess.

I was shaken back to reality by the sound of the prince yelling for one of his servants. Did I want to marry a man who was catered to day and night? I was attracted to his grand life because it felt familiar: being with a man whom everyone wanted to please. Most nights were spent in private town homes that had been converted into restaurants with small casinos upstairs. I found the long dinners we had inane and was growing tired of this life. The royals, however, took it very seriously. The prince liked to eat at Burger King late at night, so on an occasional midnight run, we pulled up with several cars. The staff retrieved his food while we remained seated in the back of one of his grand black Bentleys. When they returned with the food and Burger King's signature paper crown, I coaxed the prince into wearing it, and we all laughed together. Moments like that seemed too rare in his life.

One day, the general and his wife told me that there had been a slight miscalculation and there were no rooms available for a Saudi princess they had invited to London as their guest. A close friend of theirs had just arrived and had taken the presidential suite at the hotel. It had two bedrooms, and they wanted to know if I could possibly use the other bedroom in his suite to get dressed so they could give my room to their visitor until they found a solution. I agreed, so we put my clothes in their room and I took my dinner dress out to take with me to the suite. The general walked me up to his friend's room. On the way, the general explained that their friend was Saudi but had grown up in the United States. He was the son of a former diplomat, a businessman, a scholar from a prestigious university, and a close friend of the king. The general knocked, and after a moment a handsome man in his early thirties opened the door.

The general made the introductions, and the Saudi took the dress from my arms. While the general waited by the door, my host walked me to the guest room, went straight into the bathroom, and turned on the shower for me. He kept his hand under the running water and asked me what temperature I liked, then left the room, closing the door behind him while I stood there with my mouth open. I took my shower and washed my hair, only to discover that the hair dryer didn't work. I put on a large white terrycloth guest robe and walked out into the living room to ask for help. In this stately living room, filled with antiques and a grand piano, were several carts of teas, pastries, and fruits, all beautifully displayed. "I thought you might like a snack," he said. It felt like a movie set. He called downstairs and made sure my problem with the hair dryer was handled promptly. We had tea, and I was mesmerized by him. He was quick-witted, extremely capable, a successful businessman, and easy to talk to. And although he traveled like royalty, he wasn't the least bit stuffy. I tried several times to end our conversation because I was afraid of being late and keeping the prince waiting. When I finally got up to leave, he said to me sternly: "You are supposed to be late. You let them wait." I sat back down.

He joined us for dinner that evening, and I was careful not to be too friendly in front of the prince. We all went to the Ritz Hotel and Casino for coffee. While I was seated next to him, my Saudi friend suddenly excused himself, got up, and didn't return. I asked the prince's driver what had happened to him. The driver told me that he had gone to the airport, where his plane was waiting to take him to a meeting in Africa. He was gone. This little incident made me realize that, being used to my flamboyant and self-made father, I was drawn to a man who was focused on his own ambitions more than to one who had been groomed to address the affairs of his state.

Life couldn't go on this way forever, with supervised visits and watchful, silent guards. After several weeks, the prince's doctor finally broached the subject: Would I consider marrying the prince? I said I thought it was best if I took some time to think and return to New York. The prince told me that he would like to visit me there and meet my father.

As I happily bounced back into my life in New York, my adventures began to feel like a fading dream. But not long after I returned, the general started phoning, and I had brief conversations with the prince. They informed me that they would be arriving the following month to stay at the Waldorf Towers. I was pleased, curious to see what it would be like to spend time with them in New York. Perhaps it would be different.

As soon as the prince arrived, he wanted to see my apartment. I had a nice little duplex in New York's West Village, but I opted instead to bring him to a corporate apartment my father kept in a building on Fifty-seventh Street in Midtown, which was more glamorous. It had a driveway, unusual for New York City, and the doormen were prepared for his arrival. The prince exited his car with plainclothes guards. They rode the elevator up to the thirty-sixth floor, walked through the well-furnished two-bedroom apartment, looked at the views, accepted no refreshments, walked back to the elevator, and left. This still strikes me as odd. The prince never commented on the residence but later told the general's wife that he liked where I lived.

Meanwhile, my father—perhaps hoping that he would be made minister of defense in Jordan through his daughter's marriage—was, without my knowledge, preparing to deliver a speech at dinner. He had made plans for us to dine at Lutèce, one of his favorite restaurants and a New York landmark. We were all meeting first at a lounge in the Waldorf. The king was also in New York, and some of his top advisers would be joining us for dinner as well. My father charmed the entire group. He was thrown, though, when the prince announced that he did not want to go to Lutèce for dinner; he wanted to go instead to Benihana, a popular Japanese chain restaurant where the chefs make a show of cooking the food at each table. My father couldn't understand why the prince would want to go to a tourist attraction for dinner, but he went along with the request. But he couldn't let the prince win completely and poked fun at the place for much of the meal.

Later in the evening, my father assumed a serious tone and began to address each guest by his formal title. He began an elaborate discourse on Jordan's military, its lack of defense, and what he thought the country needed. They all nodded, not quite knowing how to respond. At the time, it seemed completely in character; in fact, I would have expected nothing less. After dinner, back at the hotel, when the doctor raised the subject of marriage to the prince with my father, he gave it about five seconds of thought. Then he announced that I was to make my own decisions. For him, the evening was over when he ended his speech.

Afterward, the doctor and I spoke, and I explained that I didn't know if marriage would be a good choice for either of us. He understood, saying that they would be leaving in a few days and asked if I would go with them to Washington, D.C. The Saudi man I had met in London was holding a birthday party for the prince there. I couldn't resist.

We drove to Washington in a motorcade and stayed at the Watergate Hotel. The dinner was in a private room in one of Washington's finest restaurants. About twenty people were present, and the prince, as the guest of honor, was seated at the head of the table. The Saudi gentleman and his family were the hosts. He told the waiters not to let anyone sit next to me except for him. I had a lovely time visiting with him, and his dynamic, independent personality further confirmed my feelings: the prince and I would probably never be a match. Yet when the doctor asked that I take a trip to visit them in Jordan, I accepted. I went back to New York and arranged to visit them the following month. My family was nervous about my traveling alone to a place that seemed so far removed from what was familiar. I cried in the car on the way to the airport, sad to leave New York and a bit frightened. I had arranged to stay at the home of family friends in Amman in order to retain a bit of independence. They had a large apartment overlooking the mountains, which were dotted with buildings instead of trees—except for the lush imported ones surrounding the royal palace.

On the day after my arrival and a good night's sleep, I met the prince at the home of his cousin for a small party. The princess lived just outside Amman, in a barren area livened up with the occasional villa. The unpaved road that led to her home was lined with what was probably a significant portion of the Jordanian army, placed there to guard her little party. When I entered the courtyard, I saw toothless bedouins holding AK-47s surrounding the prince. They were a bit intimidating in their long white cotton tunics, sandals, colorful headdresses, and wide leather belts lined with bullets. Their hands rested comfortably on their guns. I decided against making any playful gestures toward the prince for fear of their misinterpreting my movements.

Fortunately, his cousin was a lively young lady, an artist with a large studio next to the pool. The prince and other guests amused themselves by teasing her about her abstract work. These people were so different from me. I tried to imagine myself doing this often, but it felt so foreign, and I couldn't imagine ever feeling at home there.

Driving away from the party, the bedouin guards hung out of the car windows like ragged dogs as we made our way along the desolate streets. The atmosphere was substantially less enticing than the *Queen Elizabeth II,* London, and New York. Once again I sat restlessly through long evenings of superficial conversation, mostly about people I didn't know, sometimes in Arabic, which I couldn't understand. I kept busy analyzing everything I saw, trying to imagine it as part of my future. I could see the influence of

Western fashion: chic young ladies parading in miniskirts, students at large coed universities who resembled the students at home. But tradition remained strong too: I noticed plenty of Jordanians cloaked in long black flowing garments frequenting the older parts of Amman, sitting on the sidewalks, selling their goods, stopping to pray. And there was room for the truly horrible: Palestinians who were living in Jordan after the 1967 war with Israel crammed into refugee camps. There was a cholera epidemic while I was there. At my request, my friends reluctantly drove me to a camp. I looked into the dead eyes of an old shepherd who held a sign begging for medicine, and I thought back to our evenings in London and the contrast between our luxuries and this war's hardship. I wasn't so naive to think that this wasn't happening in other places in the world, including in my own country, but here it seemed especially exaggerated.

One day I drove off with a friend through the sweltering heat of the Jordanian desert to the ruins of Petra, an ancient city inhabited in 2500 B.C., located several hours south of Amman. It is known as the Rose-Red City because its temples and tombs were carved out of the red sandstone mountains. Upon arrival, we stood in front of an imposing mountain with a narrow opening not quite large enough for a car to pass through. Two nearby bedouins approached and skillfully bargained with us for the use of their camels. They laughed as we awkwardly climbed on and began our mile-long trek down the dusty path to the ruins. This was the only way to gain access, which had naturally protected the inhabitants from outside invaders. Our first glimpse was of a temple, intricately carved out of the rust-colored mountains. We got off our camels and climbed to the royal tombs, the Temple of the Winged Lions, and the house of Caiaphas, the high priest, and then sat in an amphitheater that once had held 8,000 people.

There were no hotels there, just a small lodge. The only other people present—besides the cave-dwelling bedouins—were a small film crew from Canada making a documentary. The crew shyly approached and asked if I would dress up in their beautiful costumes and play the silent role of an ancient queen. For two days I wore layers of chiffon veils, rode camels, and walked barefoot, weaving in and out of the ornate columns that supported a portico. I wondered if this ancient city was what had pulled me to Jordan. Maybe I was thousands of years too late for the role I would have really enjoyed.

Two weeks had passed since my arrival, and I felt it was time to go home. This adventure had run its course. I was homesick: I missed New York, my family, my friends, and my culture. The prince and his entourage were gracious about my decision to leave—they seemed trained not to reveal their emotions too deeply—and I was grateful for the wonderful experiences I'd shared with them. Several weeks after returning to the States, I received a phone call from the general: he was visiting and wanted to see me. We arranged to meet for lunch, during which he asked if I was sure about my decision to stay in New York. I replied that I was.

Fifteen years later, I was sitting in the lobby of the Four Seasons Hotel in Washington, D.C., having tea. A man walked past me with a group trailing him by a few steps. I couldn't see his face, but the procession had the look, often seen in Washington, of an entourage accompanying a head of state. When he turned to sit, I saw it was the prince. As I approached him, his guards jumped up and were a bit surprised when he greeted me and held my hands. The rest of the group stood as we took a few steps to the side. The first question he asked was if I was single. When I said I was, he wanted to know how I had managed to stay single for so long. I explained I hadn't, but that I was just divorced. He laughed. He said he was traveling with his wife and children. When I asked him where they were, he indicated a beautiful woman sitting on the other side of the room with two children and their uniformed nannies. His wife seemed isolated, alone. Her life could have been mine, I thought. I knew I had made the right decision.

CHAPTER THREE

Meeting Marwan

MY TRAVELS WITH THE PRINCE HADN'T LED TO ROMANCE, but they were eye-opening. After my brief flirtation with royalty, I decided to pursue my interest in the Middle East more earnestly. At the time, I was a graduate student in psychology and clinical social work at Adelphi University, taking classes on Long Island and interning in Manhattan. The idea of Washington, D.C., appealed to me. I didn't know anyone there, but I wanted to meet people who were part of the diplomatic community and involved in global politics. I proposed to Adelphi that I work with a nonprofit organization in Washington and write a master's thesis on the stereotyping of Arabs in high school history textbooks. They agreed, so I made an appointment with the National Association of Arab Americans (NAAA), an organization made up primarily of Lebanese Christians at the time, which represented the interests of Arab Americans on Capitol Hill. We had a successful meeting, and they decided to support my efforts. They suggested I work with a Lebanese American senator, James Abourzek of South Dakota, who wanted to conduct a similar study.

We set up study groups made up of Americans and Lebanese Americans from various academic and professional backgrounds to review the textbooks. The study highlighted negative stereotypes of Arabs in the coverage of the Israeli-Palestinian conflict. Our work resulted in local school districts' changing their current textbooks to more balanced teaching tools that we recommended. When the study was complete, the NAAA offered me a job in media affairs. I would serve as a liaison between Arab Americans and New York TV networks, enabling me to travel frequently between the two cities.

I enjoyed Washington and the opportunities to form ties with people from all over the world. My father saw my move as a social opportunity and visited often. He enjoyed accompanying me to work-related embassy parties and insisted on providing an apartment for me that I never could have afforded otherwise, so he still felt that he had control over my life. He was still the patriarch who took care of his family, particularly his only daughter.

Over time, I became friendly with people who worked at the Arab League offices down the street from the NAAA. The Arab League, also called the League of Arab States, is an organization that functions like a mini–United Nations, representing twenty-three countries from the Middle East and North Africa, including Saudi Arabia, Lebanon, Syria, Kuwait, Jordan, Egypt, and Tunisia. Together they coordinate political and economic policies and discuss matters of common concern. I often attended gatherings given by the Arab League in Washington. The name Marwan Kanafani, the Arab League's director in New York, kept coming up, especially among women. I was told he was very handsome and charming, a political dynamo with movie star charm.

As luck would have it, an event was coming up in New York at the United Nations, hosted by the Arab League. I was planning to be there on business, so the Arab League's lawyer, Bob Thabit, and his wife, Vivian, asked me to attend with them. Several of my friends from Washington were coming in for the event and staying at Marwan's apartment, and we arranged to meet at the end of the evening. It was a glamorous event, attended by women in elegant gowns and men in tuxedos, held in a concert hall at the U.N. building. In the receiving line, I saw a striking man standing next to the Arab League ambassador, Clovis Maksoud. I knew it had to be Marwan. He was exceptionally handsome, with tanned skin, silver hair, and a chiseled face. He looked particularly distinguished in his formal attire, the ultimate dashing diplomat.

While waiting in line, my hosts asked if I knew Marwan. When I said I didn't, they told me he was Palestinian, once the goalkeeper for the Egyptian national soccer team, previously married to a popular Egyptian actress and the brother of famed novelist Ghassan Kanafani, who had been assassinated in 1972 in Beirut. It was quite a résumé. He was friendly when we were introduced, and after he left the receiving line, he followed me throughout the reception, trying to strike up a conversation. I kept a polite distance. I imagined he was someone like my father—a devourer of women.

When the event ended, my friends told me that Marwan would be coming with us to the UN Plaza Hotel for drinks. There were ten of us, including a newscaster from Boston who had flown in to be Marwan's date for the evening. Marwan was the axis around whom everyone else revolved. He was outgoing and opinionated, and he commanded the attention of our entire group, expounding on everything from politics to religion. If anyone's opinion differed from his, his response was so abrasive that it bordered on humorous. People laughed—I assumed out of fear of confrontation. Clearly it would be hard to win any sort of debate with him. I had to admit that I was impressed. He was smart, funny, confident, and charismatic. I was a spectator, only twenty-six, he was seventeen years older. I watched him closely, assessing that he had all the deadly charms.

I was invited to have dinner the next evening with the same group of friends. They asked me to meet them at Marwan's apartment, and we would go to dinner from there. When I arrived, it seemed that he'd orchestrated the meeting. His date had flown back to Boston, and he mentioned several times that their relationship was casual. I felt a twinge of excitement at his interest, but my instincts told me to keep a distance.

It was a brisk autumn evening, and everyone huddled together in the crisp air as we walked to dinner. Marwan had to be the center of attention again. No one resisted this; they treated him as if he were still a soccer star. He loved to provoke arguments. The more he berated people, the harder they laughed. He was passionate about politics and knowledgeable about every part of the world, whether it was a current event or a historical fact. He made tremendous efforts to lure me into one of his political arguments, but I remained passive and quiet. I admired his passion, but his unpredictability made me feel unsafe.

After dinner, we all walked back to his house, where Marwan promised to serve brandy to his chilled guests. I turned down the brandy, but my friends joined him for a drink before quietly disappearing to their rooms. Marwan insisted that I stay, so we sat on his living room floor and talked. We spoke about my trip to the Middle East and about my family. He told me about his former wife, his children, and funny stories from his days as a soccer player. He did most of the talking, which is the way Marwan liked it.

Hours passed, and the sun came up. In the early morning light, we were still lounging on the floor. Our friends joined us as they woke, and we spent the next day together at his house. Issa, a 300-pound Egyptian driver and bodyguard for the Arab League, periodically checked in on us and brought us food from various neighborhood restaurants. "Captain Marwan" is how Issa referred to him, a throwback from his years as a goalie. Marwan loved hearing Issa say that he had been the most famous man in Egypt, even more revered than President Nasser. Issa told us about a riot Marwan started at a stadium when he didn't agree with the referee's ruling. He described how Marwan looked at the grandstands and, with one wave of his hand, invited thousands of fans to swarm the field in protest. I was weakening.

In the evening, after our friends left to go back to Washington, Marwan asked me to stay. He said I could have my own room; he simply did not want me to go. He seemed vulnerable and sincere. By this time, I didn't want to leave either, but I was reluctant. I would not become like my father's many girlfriends. I told Marwan this directly. He insisted that I was misreading him, that his intentions were good.

I liked that he wasn't afraid to state what he wanted, and I agreed to stay—in my own room, as he had offered. I was charmed by Marwan over the next few days, and he told me that he wanted to see me every day. He told me he wouldn't see the woman from Boston or anyone else. I prolonged my stay in New York and worked from there, and Marwan and I enjoyed the next few weeks together. He courted me with a passion. He sent drivers to get me and dispatched his bodyguard to take care of me. He held dinners at great restaurants with interesting guests. He had an exciting and active social life, and he wanted me with him everywhere he went. I found this restrictive but flattering. I thought it was an indication of how much he cared for me, and this security was something I longed for. He seemed solid, dependable. He kept his word and was serious about having a relationship. The feeling that someone would always be there was comforting. I began to believe that underneath the movie star facade was a man who was caring, kind, and protective.

My life began to revolve around Marwan's activities. I eventually left my job at the NAAA and accompanied Marwan while he was entertaining his visitors, which usually included his favorite pastime: discussing politics. We didn't have many of the same interests. I enjoyed museums, film, theater—which weren't of any interest to him; he enjoyed global politics, of which I knew little. He was comfortable in the environment he had created for himself, with friends from his part of the world, and he didn't like to move out of that comfort zone. Although I would have preferred that he share some of my interests, I only cared that he wanted me with him.

Two months after we met, he traveled to Tunis for an Arab League meeting. He wanted me to stay at his apartment while he was gone. This seemed only natural, since I had been staying there anyway. He called often to make sure I didn't leave. He seemed to worry constantly. He wanted to know I was home, safe. The more he did this, the more I thought he was in love with me.

When he returned, the attention he gave me continued. He still wanted me to spend all my time with him, did not want me to go anywhere without him or see my friends. I did invite a friend over on occasion, but the atmosphere was tense because my friend had little in common with Marwan. I did try sometimes to bring him into my world. One day, while walking by the Frick Collection on Fifth Avenue, which houses an outstanding private collection of art, I asked him to step inside. We weren't in any rush, and I wanted to show him where I had spent much of my teenage life, reading in the grand atrium. He refused. I opened the door. *Please,* I begged him, *just come in for a moment.* He wasn't interested. He didn't want to learn about the art and culture of countries outside his region. The European countries and Great Britain had occupied the countries where he was raised. He understood their political stances and he knew their history, but he couldn't bring himself to admire their art.

Meanwhile, a steady flow of diplomats came from the Middle East for meetings at the United Nations. They were well-mannered, highly educated men, all of them respectful and formal toward me. We went out for dinners with them, and though much of the conversation was in Arabic, I never complained that I couldn't understand. Sometimes I sat for hours in suites at the UN Plaza Hotel while heads of state and their bodyguards played cards, casually leaving their weapons lying on tables. If I wanted to have dinner with friends during their card games, Marwan protested, insisting that I stay. I was often the only woman present during many of these gatherings, which made me feel particularly special to Marwan. I usually sat quietly in a corner and read a book, waiting for Marwan to finish his visit. Sometimes he asked me to bring him something. This was my job: to sit and wait until he needed anything. I sometimes wondered why I was agreeing to his rules, but I was happy to be with him, even at this price. I admired his sense of humor, his strength, his intelligence. He was knowledgeable about so many things, and he was wholly devoted to his purpose in life: finding a homeland for the Palestinians.

Vanessa Redgrave, who had taken an interest in the Palestinian people, came to Marwan's one evening for dinner with several other friends. As they discussed the Israeli-Palestinian conflict, I listened much more than I spoke, as usual. At one point, Marwan decided to make my silence the brunt of his jokes, sarcastically telling me, in front of everyone, not to talk so much. I was embarrassed and walked into another room. Marwan followed me and told me he was sorry and also told me, for the first time, that he loved me. I was confused by these dueling emotions—hurt and love—but I accepted both. I was not like the other women he knew—mostly the wives of his friends who would come to his apartment from work, a constant crowd of them. They would sit all evening arguing with him. I never challenged him. I didn't know how.

One day Marwan heard me speaking to my father on the phone. He was coming to New York and wanted to take me out for dinner. Marwan asked if he could meet him. I thought this was a good indication of Marwan's seriousness about our relationship. I had not mentioned Marwan to my father, and Marwan knew little about him. I let my father know there was a man I wanted him to meet. He seemed a bit surprised and then asked me questions. I guess he was impressed enough by Marwan's position and his past that he agreed to the date.

On the evening of my father's arrival, Marwan and I stood in front of the UN Plaza Hotel waiting for him. He pulled up in a limousine, stepping out with his coat draped over his shoulder and a beautiful girl on each arm. He always had a date, usually very young. I disliked it, not so much because I had anything against the girls; I just didn't like the way he acted in front of them. He told the same stories over and over, and they were his road show. We went into the bar for drinks. Somehow, within the first few minutes of the conversation, my father questioned Marwan about his diplomat status and found out that he didn't have to pay taxes. My father wanted to know how *he* could become a diplomat as well. He engaged everyone at the bar, walked around talking to people and making them laugh. Marwan and he clearly liked each other. The three of us planned to have dinner together the next evening.

The following night, Marwan was willing to let my father take center stage. Things were going smoothly until he announced, "I really like your daughter." Expecting my father to be pleased, Marwan took another sip of his drink, enjoying the bond he felt they were forming. My father had that look in his eye, a look I knew well. He exploded: "Do you think you are doing me a favor by telling me that you *like* my daughter? I don't need you to tell me you *like* my daughter. Many men can say they like my daughter—that's not telling me anything! If you tell me you want to marry my daughter, *then* you are telling me something! I don't care that you 'like' my daughter!" Marwan tried to explain himself, only to be interrupted by, "I could put ten men like you in my hip pocket!" There was no use trying to break up the clash. I have to admit that I enjoyed my father's strong stand, because it elevated my sense of pride. Once my father had the upper hand and Marwan was on the defensive, my father began to back down, secure in his position.

When the two of us returned home, Marwan, an excellent cook, prepared one of his favorite native yogurt dishes for my father, packing him a portion to take home with him on the plane, a very Middle Eastern gesture. The next day, the three of us stood on the street shivering while my father's car waited to take him to the airport. He hugged Marwan, a subtle way of letting Marwan know that it was okay to pursue me. I knew my father liked him. If he hadn't, he wouldn't have bothered to say goodbye. Marwan was someone about whom my father could spin grand tales, and that was probably the most important criterion for a potential son-in-law.

The following week, Marwan and I went to my mother and stepfather's house on Long Island for dinner, the home they had lived in since they married twenty years earlier. My mother loved her domestic life, and my stepfather enjoyed working around the house in his spare time. Upon entering their home, visitors immediately sensed its order, its roots. Its history was told through photographs of the children during holidays, birthdays, and graduations. My mother sat playing the piano in the living room when we arrived, initially unaware of our presence. She seemed peaceful and content, the opposite of my father and the chaos he created. She cooked a Lebanese dinner for Marwan and talked about her culture and her relatives. Marwan liked her simple life, her strong commitment to her home, her husband, and my younger brother and sister. I was blessed that all the siblings from both my mother's and father's second marriages enjoyed a close bond. My mother liked Marwan for appreciating these things.

The following week was Thanksgiving. I planned to have dinner at my mother's house, but Marwan couldn't make it because he had out-of-town guests. We received a call during dinner that Fahimi, my beloved great-grandmother, had died. She was ninety-seven and had been in failing health. She never had the chance to meet Marwan, and I wondered if he could ever be the kind of friend to me she had been. When I told him about Fahimi, he was indifferent and cold, saying she had lived a long life, that there was nothing to be upset about.

It was as though I had no past. My world continued to shrink. My friends asked me why I wasn't seeing them, and I made excuses. I did start to bring some of my things to Marwan's home, including a painting of myself, done when I was in Jordan. I wanted to show Marwan, innocently telling him that a well-known male artist had painted my portrait and had given it to me as a gift. In the painting, I am reclining on a sofa, in a full-length dress, leaning against pillows painted in fantastic Moroccan designs. I have many strands of gold jewelry hanging from my neck, all painted in rich gold leafing. It looked like one of those wonderful pieces Matisse had done during his years in Tangiers, and I was proud of it. But Marwan was upset that it was painted by a man and didn't want it in his house. So to appease him, I put the painting in storage. I eventually told him that I threw the painting away.

I dealt with this predicament by focusing on his good qualities. I liked that he seldom sat still, was always on the move and doing something exciting. Marwan surprised me with a trip to Paris for the New Year. His friends had invited several couples and their family members as their guests to the elegant Plaza Athénée Hotel, a throwback to those glamorous days with the prince. On the elevator ride to our room, I commented that it was nice to be in Paris. He became angry that I hadn't said that it was nice to be in Paris "with him." This took me hours to resolve. I began to learn that I had to guard my words, always including him and leaving out references to anyone else. Marwan was pleasant for the rest of the trip, happy to be with his friends. He took me shopping and even let me go off to the Louvre by myself. He knew how to temper control with kindness. I enjoyed his friends, the dinners at beautiful restaurants, and the party they threw at Régine's, the famous Parisian nightclub, for New Year's Eve. I rationalized that although Marwan was asking me to leave a lot behind, he was also offering me many new experiences.

I was surrendering to his seduction. I'd become entranced by him and his world. It surprised me that he was the opposite of my father when it came to women. He did not have a flirtatious nature and didn't pursue other women. The significance of this almost overrode other doubts that I had about our relationship. He made his commitment to me very clear, even in public. I didn't think Marwan would ever leave me if we married, and I believed he would be a dependable father if we had children.

One day, about six months after we met, while sitting in Marwan's house waiting for him to come home, I received a call from his secretary. She asked me a question about my engagement party. My engagement party? I knew nothing about it. It turned out that Hala Maksoud, the wife of the ambassador of the Arab League, was throwing an engagement party for us. I was taken aback, of course, and asked her if Marwan was aware of it. He was. It was to take place in two days. I confronted Marwan when he got home. He responded by telling me what time the party would start. My excitement overrode my surprise. He assumed I would marry him. He was right. I called my father, who flew in just in time for the dinner.

The party was held at a posh New York restaurant in Beekman Towers, across from the United Nations. Many of Marwan's friends were in town for a global summit. A group of thirty ambassadors and dignitaries filled the room. All of the guests were male, except for two of my girlfriends and the Arab League ambassador's wife. It was more formal than festive. If not for the dim lighting and the glowing candles, the party would have resembled a U.N. conference. Each guest stood in turn and made a speech about the notion of love. Their words were rich, full of romance and poetry. The foreign minister of the PLO, Farouk Kadoumi, also known as Abu Lutaf, presented me with my engagement ring. As with many of my new acquaintances, I didn't know who he was until I happened to see him one evening on the news. I felt I was being officially initiated into Marwan's circle of friends.

Right after the engagement, my father insisted Marwan and I take a trip to see him at his home in Newport Beach, California. While we were there, one of my closest childhood friends, a boy who grew up in the house next door to my mother and was now living in California, came over to visit us. Marwan said hello and then decamped to a different room, refusing to interact with him. Angry that I had a male friend, he gave me the silent treatment, which he continued throughout the remainder of our trip. My brother, Mark, who was in law school in San Diego, drove up to Newport Beach to meet Marwan. Mark wasn't one to pay attention to his attire; his wardrobe was pretty much confined to Yankees regalia. Before he came, my father had told him several times that he had to dress nicely for dinner. (If my father didn't like the way you were dressed, you could *not* eat dinner at his table.) Mark stopped at my father's house on the way to meet us at the restaurant and dipped into my brother Jeff's wardrobe to find something to wear.

Mark arrived as we were about to begin our meal. He and Marwan shook hands. Mark's shoes caught Marwan's eye, and he commented he had just bought the same shoes in France. I saw Mark go slightly pale. Then Marwan noticed Mark's suit and commented that he also had the same one, leading to the observation that Mark was wearing all of Marwan's clothes. My father demanded to know where Mark had gotten the outfit. It turned out that when Mark went looking for clothes to wear, he had no idea that Marwan's clothes were hanging in Jeff's closet too. He had come to meet Marwan dressed from head to toe in his clothing! When we realized what happened, my brother and I burst out laughing. Marwan wasn't so amused.

Although Marwan and I rarely discussed our internal worlds, I knew there were two things that tugged at his heart: the Palestinian situation, and the death of his brother Ghassan. The two were closely related.

Marwan was born in Palestine in 1938. Ten years later, after the end of World War II, the U.N. adopted a resolution to partition the region of Palestine and carve out a homeland for the Jews. As a result, the State of Israel was declared in May 1948. Arabs resisted the declaration and fought for the land that they considered to be theirs. After a battle, the Arabs lost additional land and half of Jerusalem. It was during this time that Marwan's family fled their home town in Palestine. They went to Lebanon, then soon moved on to Syria and lived there as Palestinian refugees. Mass migrations of Jews followed, and the region has remained tumultuous ever since. In 1967, the Six Day War resulted in Israel's acquiring and occupying the West Bank of Palestine and the Gaza Strip and the other half of Jerusalem.

Marwan's brother, a famous novelist who was a major influence on modern Arab literature, wrote about the hardships of life under occupation and the moral dilemmas people face during war. I thought I could better understand Marwan by reading about Ghassan and his experiences.

I started to read Ghassan's translated literature. I found his story "Land of the Sad Oranges," which describes a family leaving Palestine in 1948 (at which time Marwan was ten and Ghassan was eight). The story is said to be based on Ghassan's life.

A cruel night, passed between the stern silence of the men and the invocations of the women. My peers, you and I, were too young to understand what the whole story was about. On that night, though, certain threads of that story became clearer. In the morning, and as the Jews withdrew threatening and fulminating, a big truck was standing in front of our door. Light things, mainly sleeping items, were being chucked into the truck swiftly and hysterically.

As I stood leaning against the ancient wall of the house I saw your mother getting into the truck, then your aunt, then the young ones, then your father began to chuck you and your siblings into the car and on top of the luggage. Then he snatched me from the corner, where I was standing and, lifting me on top of his head, he put me into the cage-like metal luggage compartment above the driver's cabin, where I found my brother sitting quietly. The vehicle drove off before I could settle into a comfortable position. My home was disappearing bit by bit in the folds of the up-hill roads leading to [Lebanon].

It was somewhat cloudy and a sense of coldness was seeping into my body. My brother, with his back propped against the luggage and his legs on the edge of the metal compartment, was sitting very quietly, gazing into the distance. I was sitting silently with my chin between my knees and my arms folded over them. One after the other, orange orchards streamed past, and the vehicle was panting upward on a wet earth. . . . In the distance the sound of gun-shots sounded like a farewell salute.

Lebanon loomed on the horizon, wrapped in a blue haze, and the vehicle suddenly stopped. The women emerged from amid the luggage, stepped down and went over to an orange vendor sitting by the wayside. As the women walked back with the oranges, the sound of their sobs reached us. Only then did oranges seem to me something dear, that each of these big, clean fruits was something to be cherished. Your father alighted from beside the driver, took an orange, gazed at it silently, then began to weep like a helpless child.

In Lebanon our vehicle stood beside many similar vehicles. The men began to hand in their weapons to the policemen who were there for that purpose. Then it was our turn. I saw pistols and machine guns thrown onto a big table, saw the long line of big vehicles coming into Lebanon, leaving the winding roads of the land of oranges far behind, and then

I too cried bitterly. Your mother was still silently gazing at the oranges, and all the orange trees your father had left behind glowed in his eyes. As if all those clean trees which he had bought one by one were mirrored in his face. And in his eyes, tears which he could not help hiding in front of the officer at the police station, were shining.

When in the afternoon we reached Sidon we had become refugees.

Despite their painful history, Marwan did tell me that he was different from his brother, sharing just one story from childhood with me. They had both snuck into a neighbor's yard and taken apples from her tree. Their father found out and decided they should be punished. From the ceiling, he hung an apple over each of their beds so they would look at it and think about what they had done. In the morning, when their father came in and asked what they had learned, Ghassan cried and said he was sorry for stealing the apple. Marwan had eaten his.

As adults, Marwan received a degree in law from the University of Cairo and played soccer while Ghassan finished his secondary education in Arabic literature at the University of Damascus. Ghassan then moved to Kuwait, where he worked as a teacher. Ghassan stayed in the Middle East and settled in Beirut, where he became the editor of an esteemed Pan-Arab newspaper, calling for Arab unity. His first novel, *Men in the Sun*, written in 1963, was adapted by the Egyptian director Tawfiq Salim into a film, *al-Makhduun. Men in the Sun* is the story of three Palestinians who attempt to escape occupied Palestine to Kuwait in the tank of a water truck. The characters represent three different generations. In the gloomy ending, they perish in their journey across the desert, a metaphor for the extinction of the Palestinian people. While the refugees are dying under the heat of the sun, they knock continuously on the wall of the tank, crying, "We are here, we are dying, let us out, let us free." The film was banned in some Arab countries for its criticism of Arab regimes. Ghassan kept the Palestinian cause moving through his stories and had great influence over his people.

On July 8, 1972, Ghassan's eighteen-year-old niece was visiting him in Beirut from Kuwait. They got into his car, planning to drive to the home of some friends. After traveling a short distance, the car exploded, booby-trapped by a bomb set off by remote control. They were killed instantly. No one claimed responsibility, but it was common knowledge at the time and then confirmed years later that it had been the Mossad, the Israeli intelligence. Ghassan was able to provoke Palestinian nationalism, which was seen as a threat. He was thirty-six years old.

Marwan was on an airplane to Beirut when the explosion occurred. The pilot, knowing he had a famous passenger, summoned him to the cockpit to break the news before landing. In the meantime, thousands of mourners had poured into the streets. From that moment on, Marwan dedicated his life to finding a solution to this conflict that senselessly killed innocent Israelis and Palestinians. His soccer days were over. These were the experiences that shaped Marwan's life and drove him.

The strains of the Palestinian-Israeli conflict never affected my own family's political beliefs. My parents and all the generations before them were from Lebanon, but my stepfather, who had been adopted, was Jewish by birth, and they had many close Jewish friends. The Middle East conflict had not colored their attitudes or beliefs whatsoever. I was forgiving of Marwan's possessive nature when I learned more about his history. I could understand that he was afraid of losing what he loved.

As time went on, I learned more about Marwan's past, although not always from him. After our engagement, Amal Abu

Sharif and Im Hassan, wives of Marwan's friends, came from Lebanon to visit us. Amal was married to Bassam Abu Sharif, a top adviser to PLO leader Yasir Arafat. She was in her thirties, slim, with a model's frame. She was dressed casually in jeans accessorized with a fashionable bag and shoes, hardly looking as if she had just stepped off a plane from Lebanon, a country shredded by civil war. Her husband had been Ghassan's best friend and had also planned to join Ghassan on his fateful car ride. A last-minute change of plans saved him.

Amal told me about the circumstances of her marriage nine years earlier. She was a Christian, and Bassam was a Muslim, and her family objected to their marriage. They requested that she not see Bassam for a month in order to reflect on whether she really wanted to marry him. She complied with her parents' orders, but she never wavered. It was during this time that Ghassan was killed. Eleven days later, on the final morning of their month-long separation, she met with Marwan and told him she would finally see Bassam that evening and tell him she still wanted to marry him.

The hours that followed did not go as planned. That afternoon, Bassam received a book in the mail. When he opened the front cover, he saw hundreds of little black wires, connected to a bomb. It exploded in his hands. The bomb had also been planted by Israeli intelligence. When the news flooded the airwaves, Amal rushed to the hospital to be by his side. Bassam had lost an eye, some of his hearing, and several fingers. She told him in his half-conscious state that she wanted to marry him and had planned to tell him that evening anyway. Bassam was afraid she was making the decision out of sympathy. Marwan was the only person who could confirm that she had made the decision before the bombing. She remained grateful to Marwan for years.

Shortly after Amal left, Im Hassan arrived. She was a slightly more conservative woman with stunning dark features. She was the widow of Ali Hassan Salameh, known as the Red Prince, a notorious jet set member of the PLO who had been pursued relentlessly by Mossad. At the time, I didn't know more than that, but I gathered that he was important, since his picture was one of the larger ones in Marwan's home. During their visit, the Red Prince's story came to light. The Red Prince and Im Hassan had two children. Then he married Georgina Risk, a Lebanese woman who had become Miss Universe. Though his marriage to Im Hassan was emotionally over, he didn't divorce her, and polygamy wasn't illegal. Marwan, however, hadn't approved of the second marriage because of his friendship with Im Hassan. In 1979, Marwan and the Red Prince were sitting in a café in Beirut while two jeeps with bodyguards waited for them to finish. Upon leaving, Marwan and the Red Prince climbed into the back of a jeep that was sandwiched between two cars of bodyguards. As they began to drive off, the Red Prince said he wanted to stop and see Georgina. Marwan refused, so he asked the driver to stop and let him out. He signaled for one of the bodyguards in the jeep behind him to ride in his place.

Marwan started to walk back to the café when he was thrown by an explosion. As he looked up, he saw the remnants of the Red Prince's car. He ran toward him, stepping over the guards' bodies, including the man who had just taken his place. The Red Prince was still breathing, and Marwan held his head in his lap. When Marwan lifted him up, he saw that the back of his head was shattered. Sirens were going off as ambulances rushed to the scene. They whisked him to a hospital, and Im Hassan quickly followed. The Red Prince died an hour later. It had been announced on the news that Marwan was killed because witnesses had seen him getting in the car with the Red Prince, and his family had already gathered in grief. It wasn't until hours later that they learned Marwan was still alive.

When I heard these stories, I felt as if I was living with a stranger. There was always a distance, a line I couldn't cross. Yet I think the distance was oddly comfortable for both of us: it kept us safe from the danger of too much intimacy.

CHAPTER FOUR

The Marriage

IN EARLY APRIL 1982, JUST SEVEN MONTHS AFTER WE met, Marwan and I decided to move to Washington, D.C. Marwan's home in New York City was constantly overflowing with visitors, and I thought that a move might bring more balance to our lives. We knew many of the same people in Washington, and I hoped that I could have a better social life, with my own friends, ones Marwan would accept. Marwan liked the idea of being able to have a small garden and grow vegetables, a virtual impossibility in the middle of Manhattan, so we went house hunting. We ended up renting a large apartment in a luxurious building in Chevy Chase, just outside the city. There wasn't a garden, but we did have a glass solarium where Marwan could grow his plants. Marwan had his post at the Arab League in New York transferred to the Washington office, and we planned a wedding and reception for a hundred people at the Four Seasons Hotel in Georgetown in June.

With so many friends and relatives coming in, preparing our new home, and getting ready for the wedding, my days were filled. In the evenings, Marwan and I visited friends, all of them Middle Eastern diplomats. These people were from different cultures, but I understood their formalities, the customary division that usually took place: men went to one room, women to another. I enjoyed the women. Some were quiet, accomplished at the art of being a diplomatic wife; others were fiery and articulate. Overall, they were warm and made me feel comfortable. I wasn't sure what my life as Marwan's wife would be like, but I knew it would be my new job. I would not pursue my own life or career; my focus would be making Marwan happy. That is what my father had taught me and what Marwan expected. I thought that little by little, I could interest him in the things I enjoyed, get him to listen to music I liked, and persuade him to socialize with some of my old friends. I was willing to give it time.

Meanwhile, Marwan's sons from his previous marriage, then thirteen and eighteen years old, who lived with their mother in Egypt, were coming to stay with us three weeks before our wedding. I would be meeting them for the first time. Marwan wanted to have a quick civil marriage service at the local courthouse prior to their arrival because he didn't want them to know that I was living with him before we were married. We went to city hall with Clovis Maksoud, the Arab League ambassador, as our witness. Marwan's desire to be legally married was a respectful gesture toward me: in the Middle East, a woman's virtue is held in the highest regard. Marwan was protecting my "reputation" not only with his sons, but with the other members of his family who would be flying in before the wedding celebration. That evening we had a small party for some friends at our new Chevy Chase apartment.

Marwan's sister and brother-in-law flew in from Kuwait with their children. She was modern and glamorous, but it was difficult to communicate due to our language barrier. Her husband was kind and helped her with their two little girls. I had seen pictures of Marwan's parents. They too were modern, his mother wearing a fashionable dress, with perfectly coiffed hair and flawless makeup. The women in his family didn't seem to live in the shadows. His brother Ghassan's two children came from Lebanon. They were well-behaved, respectful children, happy to be among their cousins. Marwan was kind and loving toward them. It warmed me to see this side of him.

The atmosphere at our house was festive and upbeat. Then, on June 3, one week before the wedding, there was an attempted assassination of Israel's ambassador in London. Although this was carried out by the Abu Nidal Organization, a radical Palestinian faction at war with the PLO, the Israeli Defense Forces retaliated by bombing PLO strongholds in Beirut, home of the PLO headquarters.

Until then, I had been completely unaware of the different Palestinian factions; I had thought there was only one organization representing the Palestinian people. The PLO had gone through many phases since its formation in 1964. It had been created to provide an organized channel for Palestinian nationalism, with a 15-member executive committee, which made policy decisions; a 60-member central committee to act as an advisory board; and a 599-member council composed of Palestinian civilians. It had gained significant strength in 1967 after the Arabs were defeated in the Six Day War and lost substantial territory to Israel. Yasir Arafat was elected chairman of the PLO that same year. Arafat's political party was called Fatah. Abu Nidal had split from Arafat back in 1974 because of Abu Nidal's terrorist activities. He tried to get the lost support of the PLO and overthrow Arafat but failed. Now the PLO was suffering the consequences of Abu Nidal's gang. On June 4 and 5, the PLO responded to the shelling by attacking the Israeli population in Galilee. On June 6, Israel invaded Lebanon with U.S. support. Following the orders of Israeli defense minister Ariel Sharon, 60,000 Israeli soldiers were sent into Lebanon.

The announced purpose of the attack was to drive the PLO away from their locations in southern Lebanon, out of range of the Israeli border. Although this had been announced as the initial aim, it was obvious that the objective was actually the destruction of the PLO in order to eliminate its threat to Israeli citizens and its political threat to the established policies of the Israeli government. This action was also supported by a large percentage of the Christian Lebanese population. A civil war had haunted Lebanon since 1975, as Palestinian supporters feuded with their enemies, primarily Lebanese Christians. The large presence of Palestinians, mostly Muslims, greatly outnumbering the Christian population, had tipped the balance of the Christian-Muslim population. Many of the Christians had aligned themselves with the Israelis and were known to be working with them to remove the Palestinians. Although there had been continued violence between Israel and the PLO since 1967, a cease-fire had been in effect for eleven months, so the Arab world was stunned by this new attack, which claimed the lives of many Palestinians and Lebanese. Now Marwan, his friends, and his family sat in front of the TV, fixated on the gruesome images.

It felt inappropriate to hold a wedding celebration during such a devastating time, but many of our relatives had already arrived. Ultimately we altered our plans, canceling the Four Seasons and settling on a more subdued gathering at our home. More of Marwan's friends came from Europe and the Middle East. They brought beautiful jewelry as gifts, as is customary. In the Middle East, there is no such thing as alimony in case of divorce, so women are given jewelry as a dowry instead. My entire family was present: brothers, sisters, my father and a young girlfriend, my mother and stepfather. Watching everyone get along was wonderful. We had two separate ceremonies, one performed by a Muslim religious sheik and one performed by a nondenominational minister. (Marwan believed that religion was a personal choice, and it didn't play a part in our marriage.)

In the midst of our celebration, the doorbell rang. The wives of the Saudi, Syrian, and Arab League ambassadors stood on my doorstep, looking frail on the fourth day of their hunger strike. The strike, staged across the street from the White House, was a protest against the Lebanon invasion. I knew some of these women from living in Washington prior to meeting Marwan, and some I'd met through him. They looked drawn and tired. Refusing any refreshments, they hugged guests in solidarity and soon returned to the large group of Arab and Jewish women who had gathered to support their position. I felt honored that they came to celebrate our marriage and was proud that both Arabs and Jews were coming together to protest this invasion. Our wedding photographer, Albert, who had covered embassy receptions his entire career, ended up taking photos of each person entering our house and saying hello to either Marwan or myself. Tellingly, not a single one of our wedding pictures is a traditional photo of Marwan and me or our families together.

After the wedding, the war became the focus of our lives. The initial shelling had turned into a full-fledged battle, with Israel refusing to give up until it successfully removed the PLO from Lebanon. Lebanon had become home to more than 300,000 Palestinian refugees since 1948. They had formed a state within a state in south Lebanon, and the PLO headquarters was stationed to the north. Our relief from this tension came from Marwan's sons and nephew, who stayed with us for the summer. Marwan loved having them with us and paid a lot of attention to them, cooking for them, taking them to sporting events and to visit our friends' teenagers. I realized that no matter where we lived, we'd always be surrounded by others. World events only exacerbated this: I'd married into a political struggle, and it would take precedence over our personal lives.

The situation in the Middle East continued to deteriorate, and the shelling of Beirut dragged on for ten violent weeks, with thousands of civilians killed. During these dark weeks, Marwan and his close network of friends and relatives held vigils and spent long nights discussing events and speculating about the future. I sat with them and listened. They appreciated my sympathy, but I was an outsider. My role was to make sure our house was run in a proper fashion and that guests were received with the appropriate Arab hospitality.

Things came to a head in September when a multinational peacekeeping force was called into Beirut and 14,000 PLO combatants were sent out of the country by Israel and the United States. It was a grim mark of defeat for Arafat and the PLO. They went into exile, taking their movable government to Tunis. On September 14, the newly appointed president of Lebanon, Bachir Gemayel, a Christian (as dictated by their constitution), was assassinated. Gemayel represented the Phalangist Party, comprising Lebanese Christians (though not all Lebanese Christians supported the party) and allies of Israel. A radical Syrian group claimed responsibility for the killing. The day after the assassination, Israel took control of the Muslim section of Beirut, where the Palestinians lived. Israel allowed the Lebanese militia, who were aligned with them, to enter two Palestinian refugee camps, Sabra and Shatila, massacring 1,400 men, women, and children. Meanwhile, in Israel, 400,000 people took to the streets in the largest demonstration in the country's history to protest the invasion and the Sabra and Shatila massacres. Defense Minister Ariel Sharon was held responsible for allowing the incidents, and after an investigation by Israel, he was forced to resign.

Marwan's mood reflected these events. He seemed both sad and angry, perhaps even lost. He had no homeland. America was his home, but not by choice. I could sympathize, but not the way his compatriots could. He came alive in the evenings when we gathered with his friends. They shared his anger and spent hours discussing how they had gotten into the situation and how they would get out. Interactions with people outside his circle became even more awkward. I invited a friend with whom I had worked at the NAAA to our home. She was a second-generation Syrian, very bright and conservative. Marwan seemed uncomfortable, unable to make small talk, and the atmosphere was tense. To break the ice, my friend and I started telling a funny story about one of her dates. One night, she'd gone out with a Saudi prince and didn't return. Her friends (me included) didn't know she was planning to take a red-eye flight to visit her parents after dinner. When she didn't return from her date, we went to the police station with her picture and reported her missing. When they contacted her family, we found out she was there. At the time it was terrible, but now we laughed at the incident. Marwan listened and then asked me to come into the other room. He had become upset and told me he wanted her to leave right away. "What kind of girl goes out with Saudi princes? Did you do the same thing!?"

Even relatively innocent incidents showed our cultural differences. We could perceive the same situation in two completely different ways. Although it was interesting to be privy to such a cloistered world, I felt lonely at times. I no longer felt like myself. Occasionally we steered away from our traditional social gatherings for a more diverse evening, such as when we were invited to a dinner party held by one of our few American friends.

The guest of honor was Robert F. Kennedy's widow, Ethel Kennedy. Marwan was seated next to her. She was completely enthralled by him. She kept yelling over to me that he was one of the most handsome and intelligent men she had ever met, and then pulled him from his seat to dance with her. She had insisted they stand on the couch and dance, and I laughed as I watched Marwan. We had a great time, and he actually enjoyed himself. Politics always loomed large, though. He had been a fan of Bobby Kennedy and didn't want to tell Ethel that he was a Palestinian, like Bobby's assassin, Sirhan Sirhan.

Some visitors brought a breath of fresh air into the house. One was Raymonda Tawil, an old friend of Marwan whose daughter would marry Arafat in 1990. Raymonda was a Palestinian who lived in Paris. When Marwan told me that she would be coming to visit, I prepared myself for another drawn-out political pow-wow. But in walked a glamorous woman, about fifteen years older than me, with blonde hair and blue eyes. Her presence filled the room. She had a dreamy quality about her and the curiosity of a child. She wanted to learn about everything, she wanted to share ideas, she wanted to talk about art and books. She had a refreshing enthusiasm for life, a desire to understand events on as many levels as she could. She also wanted to know about hair and fashion, telling me she loved to re-create herself, not out of dissatisfaction but out of a sense of adventure. She was delightful and filled me with energy, and Marwan respected her intellect too.

Other friends had told me about Raymonda's past. She had been one of the first people to try to create a dialogue with the Israelis in the 1970s. She was a journalist, and when she lived under occupation in the West Bank town of Nablus, her home was known as a political salon, a place where Israelis and Palestinians could gather for conversation. Raymonda spoke Hebrew and had many Israeli friends because she had gone to boarding school with Israelis as a young girl.

Because Raymonda had tried to bridge the gap between Israelis and Palestinians in the 1970s, she had been considered a traitor by some of her people and wasn't trusted by the Israelis. For example, in 1984 her car was blown up in front of her West Bank home. Responsibility for the incident was never claimed. She was jailed, tortured, and lived under house arrest for several months. She was the subject of many books and plays. I was shocked that she never spoke about these things. She was the ideal blend of femininity and strength. I wanted to tell her that I was strong and independent too; I wanted to whisper this great secret to her, but I couldn't let Marwan hear me.

Another woman who deeply impressed me was King Hussein of Jordan's first wife, Queen Dina. I had met her at a dinner at the Mayfair Hotel in Washington. Marwan and I were rushing through the lobby when I spotted a woman, very elegant, hair in a French twist, wearing a leopard print dress, speaking on a pay phone. As I stared at her, Marwan ran over and said hello. Strutting back toward me, he told me who she was. A queen on a pay phone? I was intrigued. I observed her and her second husband, Salah Tamari, at the next table at dinner. She seemed warm and gracious, happily obliging photographers and the continual flow of people interrupting her dinner. At the end of the evening, Marwan told me that she and her husband would be coming to visit the following evening.

They were a striking couple. Salah was tall and handsome. He had led the Palestinians in battle against Queen Dina's former husband, the king. She met him just before this. They fled to

Lebanon, and years later, during the 1982 Israeli incursion into their village, he was rounded up and jailed. Queen Dina managed to free him and 8,000 other prisoners when she negotiated one of the largest prisoner exchanges in the history of the world. They were romantic figures who both loved literature. They saw themselves as Odysseus and Penelope in Greek mythology, because she was always waiting for him to return from battles or from jail.

I later went with Queen Dina to see an exhibit of antique silver at the Smithsonian. Many of the pieces were on loan from ruling families and palaces in the Middle East. As we walked through the gallery's rooms, we gazed at the silver treasures encased in glass with their origins posted below. After reading about the pieces, Queen Dina would often turn to me with excitement and exclaim, "Oh, this belonged to my uncle!" or "This belonged to my grandfather!" Of course, she was within earshot of other museum-goers, who stared at her.

After the museum outing, we joined our husbands. I was told we would be visiting some of Salah's friends. We drove deep into a rural part of Maryland, to a very small house. The house was crammed with men who had been political prisoners with Salah. They had gathered to see the queen and thank her. They stood and saluted Dina, and she greeted each one and then went into the kitchen, where she rolled up her sleeves and helped female family members cook.

By that time, Marwan and I were anxiously awaiting the birth of our first child. When I gave birth to a beautiful little girl on his birthday, we named her Deena. Having a daughter was a shock to Marwan. He already had two sons, and I think he assumed he would have more. He was fascinated by her and for the first few months referred to her as "the girl." I had to keep reminding him that she had a name. It took him a while to feel comfortable playing with her.

The baby kept me busy and happy, and she was a great joy to both of us. I had little time to think about much else. My mother and stepfather were frequent visitors, as were my brothers. Fourteen months later, I became pregnant with our precious son, Tarik. We were thrilled with our children, and as time went on, it became clear that they were our only common interest.

My father was enjoying the marriage, or at least the parties that went along with it. One evening we took him to a cocktail party for Philip Habib at Ambassador Maksoud's house. Philip was the special White House envoy to the Middle East. He had just returned from a trip to Lebanon and agreed to be the guest of honor at the party on the condition that he wouldn't have to address the crowd. My father strolled into the sunken living room, packed elbow to elbow with Washington power brokers, singled out Philip from across the room, and began to yell: "Hi, Phil, how's the family? Haven't seen you in such a long time!" Philip had to respond, thinking he must know my father. My father proceeded to tell everyone, in front of Philip, that they had gone to school together. Halfway through the gathering, he began to make loud requests for Philip to say a few words, exactly what Philip was promised he wouldn't have to do. My father rallied the crowd into a chant, demanding that he address the crowd. Philip finally succumbed, my father privately enjoying his little game.

The next day the ambassador's wife called me, quite excited, and asked why I never told her that my father and Phil had known each other from school. When I told her that my father had never seen him before in his life, she was so shocked and amused that she called all of our friends and repeated the story.

My dad loved Marwan and his status. He wouldn't have understood that Marwan did not see me as a separate person; after all, neither did he. My efforts to expand our social circles or pursue other activities met with his disapproval.

I wondered about Marwan's first marriage, which he never talked about. I knew his ex-wife was a famous actress in Egypt. She came to visit us shortly after our daughter Deena was born. Their son Hakam was studying at the University of Maryland at the time. She was beautiful and very kind. I invited her for dinner with Marwan's son. Her English wasn't good, but she insisted that Marwan and their son refrain from speaking Arabic because she wanted to include me. She was interested in Hollywood and planned to visit the Los Angeles studios after our visit. Marwan told her he couldn't understand why she would do such a thing alone and tried to talk her out of it. She didn't engage in an argument; she just nicely said she was going because she wanted to, and that was it.

More and more, I began to feel that my marriage was weakening. I was yearning for a life once again filled with my friends and my American culture. I had agreed to the marriage on Marwan's terms, and now I wanted to change those terms. Tension grew between us as I was trying to change the rules in the middle of the game. I felt invisible, but I didn't want to argue, I didn't want to be divorced like my parents.

Plus, he was a good father. Marwan loved to be with the children. But he started to travel more. Like his peers, he was accustomed to living in two worlds, one political and one familial. Marwan missed his contact with the Palestinian delegations that he used to see in New York when they came to the United Nations. Playing from the sidelines in Washington frustrated him. He started to take trips more often to Tunis, where he had the chance to renew his relationship with Arafat and the other Palestinians now stationed there. He always seemed happy when he was leaving to travel. Meanwhile I began to take trips with the children to my father's home in Newport, California, when Marwan traveled. I spent more time with my brothers, and they took me to concerts and dinners. They wanted to involve me in my father's businesses. I went to museums in Los Angeles and walked down its streets, gazing into trendy boutiques. I was starting to feel alive again.

As our relationship grew more distant, Marwan's relationship with Arafat grew stronger. He told me that Arafat listened to him, respected him, and liked that he was not afraid to oppose him. They were hopeful about their political future. Marwan attended meetings with Arafat that could lead to a peaceful resolution of the Palestinian-Israeli conflict. Whenever Marwan was home in Washington, Arafat called constantly, wanting to know when he would be back in Tunis. Sometimes Arafat got on the phone with me to say hello. He said that he hoped we would meet, and then tease Marwan by referring to him as *Nugut*, an Arabic term for a difficult person. Arafat was becoming dependent on Marwan and wanted him by his side all the time.

In 1990 we decided to separate for the summer. We agreed that the children and I would go to California and stay with my father while Marwan was in Tunis. My summer in California was wonderful. I saw friends and went to dinner with them. I could hear Marwan's voice in my head, condemning me for being out. I realized I was constantly anticipating how he might react. I was far from him, but I wasn't free. What had happened to that confident young woman? I wanted to find her again. The loneliness and yearning for the person I once was finally began to surpass my need for security.

I met Marwan back in Washington at the end of the summer. He seemed to have enjoyed the summer as much as I did. I suggested we have a legal separation. He was surprised, and I don't think he believed that I had the confidence to make such an audacious request. He would have preferred to keep our home together and our marital status the same; he would just spend much of his time in Tunis. This was the Middle Eastern way: just to live separately, spend time apart, but still keep the legal marriage intact. This helped avoid the stigmas of divorce. We moved forward with the formal separation, and he left for Tunis again. I clung to a fantasy that one day our marriage could work, that we could be friends, two people who respected each other.

I moved into a comfortable apartment with my children, off Washington's elegant Foxhall Drive, and Marwan stayed in Tunis. My father helped us financially, which gave him great pleasure. I opened a branch office for his warranty company in Washington and worked on marketing campaigns. At last I started making friends with people who shared my interests. I went to lectures at the Smithsonian. I took trips to SoHo in New York City and reveled in the pleasure of meeting friends at cafés and going to galleries. I was breathing again; I was feeling stronger. But Marwan didn't seem particularly talkative when he would call, and our conversations were short and to the point. Yet I still wanted to go back to him, as a stronger person. Maybe we could meet on new ground. I met an old friend from college in New York. Her words stung me: "You are still trying to capture the unobtainable man like your father. They will never see you; they can only see themselves." It was true, but it wasn't enough to stop me from trying again.

Marwan started coming to Washington for work that he was doing as part of a team handling peace negotiations between Palestinians and Israelis. He started visiting me and the children. He seemed more content now that he had an active role in this important work. He was calmer, more respectful, willing to try things that I liked. My magical thinking led me to agree to move back in with him. I had visions of a new type of relationship. I found the events surrounding the peace negotiations interesting and enjoyed entertaining many of the people involved. Mary

King, who was special adviser to President Carter and had global responsibility for the Peace Corps, came to our house one evening and made suggestions to members of the Palestinian negotiation team on how to promote peaceful images of themselves in the American media. It was Christmastime, and she suggested having the mayor of Bethlehem, who was visiting, go to the White House and attend the lighting of the Christmas tree. She suggested that the press film the negotiating team at the National Archives, reading the Bill of Rights. The men all looked at her as though her ideas were absurd. They had no concept of the importance of public relations.

Maybe my ideas about our marriage were absurd too. It was even more strained now with the demands of my work. And when an old friend visited, increasing the atmosphere of tension with Marwan, I saw no reason for us to return to our old patterns. I was disappointed and sad that it couldn't be different. I respected Marwan intellectually and as a father, but our marriage no longer worked.

CHAPTER FIVE

The Peace Signing

I CONTINUED TO LIVE IN WASHINGTON WITH MY CHIL-
dren while Marwan moved full time to Tunis. We didn't see each
other much over the next year and a half, speaking only occasionally over the phone. We rarely discussed our relationship, and it
seemed we had both started enjoying our separate lives. Marwan
traveled all winter with Arafat, developing a close and trusting
relationship, eventually becoming his senior adviser and spokesman. Fortunately, Tarik and Deena appeared unaffected by the
separation. They knew Marwan was away working, which they
were used to, and I didn't talk to them about the separation. I
remembered the pain I'd felt when my own parents divorced. It
wasn't uncommon for fathers in our circle to spend long periods

of time overseas. I was also careful to keep the children's lives consistent. They continued going to the same school and saw the same friends. They spent time in Tunis with their father during their summer vacation, staying at the villa of an American woman and her family. We talked on the phone often, and they seemed to be enjoying themselves.

Marwan had become increasingly involved with the peace negotiations between the Palestinians and Israelis. An agreement was finally reached in August 1993. The Oslo Accords, officially known as the Declaration of Principles (DOP), outlined a process in which Palestinian self-rule would take place in stages over the next five years. The agreement included a withdrawal of Israeli forces from parts of the Gaza Strip and West Bank, the rights of the Palestinians to self-govern through the creation of the Palestinian National Authority, a Palestinian police force, and economic cooperation between Israel and Palestine. Israel would maintain control over the protection of Israelis living in settlements in the West Bank, border security, and freedom of movement on roads. After the five-year interim agreement, other issues would be discussed, such as Jerusalem, refugees, and settlements. Marwan played a key role in this process, writing Arafat's speeches and advising him on policies and strategies.

The DOP were met with mixed reactions. In Israel, the left wing supported them, while the right wing did not. In Palestine, Arafat's party, Fatah, accepted the accords, but Hamas, Arafat's opposition (largely seen as the more extremist party), did not. With the hope that peace could prevail, Israeli and Palestinian representatives were to sign Letters of Mutual Recognition on the White House lawn on September 13, 1993. Mahmoud Abbas, a central figure and main architect of the peace accords, would represent Palestine. It was decided at the last minute that Arafat would also come to the United States for the signing, after being considered persona non grata for thirty years. (Technically he was allowed back into the country after 1988, when the PLO formally renounced the use of terrorism.) But he'd never been formally invited, and according to Marwan, there hadn't been any formal dialogue between the United States and the PLO.

I had been in touch with friends at the Palestinian mission in Washington and they told me that they had just been alerted that Arafat—and therefore Marwan—would be attending the ceremony. This was completely unexpected, as only Arafat's representatives were scheduled to attend. On the spur of the moment, I decided to take my daughter to the ANA Hotel, where they were to arrive. (My son, being a bit younger, stayed home.) I'd never met Arafat in person.

I'd been told that Suha Arafat was scheduled to accompany her husband. Just a few months earlier, they had gone public with their marriage after living in secrecy for three years. Arafat had been afraid that the marriage would cause too much controversy. It was hard for me to believe that a man who always walked with the threat of death at his side would be worried about others' opinions when it came to his love life. More than that, I wondered what kind of woman would marry Arafat. Who was capable of penetrating his enigmatic shield? I knew only sketchy details. She was the daughter of Raymonda Tawil and a Christian. Raised in Palestine, she had lived in Paris and held a master's degree from the Sorbonne. I could tell from conversations with Marwan, who would grunt at the mention of her name, that Arafat's inner circle wasn't particularly fond of her. She was seen as a threat, and she softened Arafat's image. After all, he had always declared to his people that he was "married to the revolution," that he was above the demands of human emotions like love. But in 1990, when he succumbed to marriage, a power stronger than any global threat had captured him.

The ANA Hotel was in a frenzy when I arrived. Helicopters zoomed overhead; Secret Service agents were everywhere; press were lining up. My daughter and I stood behind a police line next to the hotel entrance as the motorcade sirens grew closer. Finally the cars swept around the corner and pulled into the hotel's circular driveway. In symphonic timing, all the car doors swung open just a few seconds before the vehicles came to a full stop. Men, all wearing suits and dark sunglasses, emerged. I called out to Marwan, who had gotten out of the first car. He ran over and instructed security to move the police line and rushed us into a hotel elevator with the Secret Service. There was hardly any time to talk in the elevator, and when the doors opened, we were greeted by a flurry of activity: the hotel floor being wired with monitors, metal detectors wheeled into place, and security clearances issued. Ambassadors, journalists, and assorted supporters were scurrying to take their places.

Marwan directed us to the presidential suite, where Suha Arafat's brother and sister were waiting for her to arrive. I knew her brother, Gabi, as he had occasionally visited us. Suha's sister, Leila, a doctor in Rome, had just arrived. We exchanged quick pleasantries and waited for Arafat, who was supposedly on his way to the suite after making a quick speech in the lobby. I left briefly to say hello to several ambassadors, who were being trailed by ABC News anchor Peter Jennings and *Nightline*'s Ted Koppel. Then I settled into a comfortable chair and waited.

Arafat entered a few moments later. He moved through the room like the eye of a storm, calm and in control, encircled by a flurry of commotion. I observed him from afar as he greeted people. He was such an iconic figure, seen as a villain by some and a hero by others. It was hard to distinguish image from reality. I recognized in him an embodiment of forty years of history: a fragile, multifaceted man. He would have been the perfect subject of a cubist painting, I thought, divided up into a vast array of colors and dimensions capturing his life better than words ever could. Marwan led my daughter and me to him. Arafat held Deena as if she were his own. He smiled at me with great kindness, and as he hugged me, I was sure he knew he had something that I would never have: my husband's complete devotion.

But where was Suha? I asked Marwan about her. "She didn't come. This is not a social event," he snapped, as if her accompanying them had been a ridiculous thought to begin with. I tried to get a friendlier, slightly more informative answer by asking some of the aides the same question, but they were all anxious to take credit for her absence, as if it were some kind of an achievement to exclude her. Meanwhile, her siblings had no idea that she wasn't showing up. It must have been a last-minute decision, I assumed, since no one had told the family that she wasn't coming. When they approached Arafat about it, he said only that there had been a change in plans. I had been told by friends that Suha was outspoken, theatrical, and inventive, so I wondered how the men surrounding her husband managed to exclude her. At any rate, there would be an empty seat in the first row on the White House lawn between Mrs. Clinton and Mrs. Rabin, wife of Israeli prime minister Yitzhak Rabin.

Meanwhile, Marwan was juggling Arafat, the press, and the White House detail in between speaking with us. I was happy to see that he seemed content and more relaxed than ever before. He was doing what he enjoyed. He was warm and loving toward our daughter and me. He was charming and handsome, reminding me of the first night I saw him in the receiving line at the United Nations twelve years earlier. I watched him and remembered what had attracted me to begin with.

He asked me if I wanted to sit in on an interview that Peter Jennings was conducting with Arafat. I said yes, of course, and was the only person present during the interview besides the camera and sound man. At one point, Jennings misplaced his contact lenses and became frantic. He called for more makeup while Arafat sat across from him calmly, all stubby beard and simple clothes, a puzzled look on his face.

At the end of the interview, when the cameras stopped rolling, Jennings snuck in a last-minute question: "Off-camera, I would like to ask you something. I was with you on your worst day, when you were defeated and had to leave Lebanon in 1982. Now I am with you on this victorious day, when you are being welcomed and treated like a hero. How does it feel to experience these extremes?" Arafat looked at Peter Jennings and delivered a line that perfectly summed up the paradox of his power: "Both days were my duty and my destiny."

When I relayed the story to Marwan and several of Arafat's advisers, each one said they'd prepared him for such a question. The men who surrounded Arafat were like children struggling to curry favor with a parent. I thought Arafat had a soft touch; at any given moment I would look at him and see the vulnerability of a child. When I mentioned this to Marwan, he warned me not to be deceived.

After the interview, people streamed through the suite, many of them our friends. They brought good wishes and Arafat's favorite gifts, like videos of "Tom and Jerry." This flow of guests continued late into the night, everyone holding their breath, hoping that nothing would go wrong before the signing scheduled for the following day. Marwan was insistent that I return in the morning. I wasn't sure if he wanted to see me or if he just wanted me to see him at work in his new role. He implied we would go to the White House for the signing. A driver took my daughter and me home and then picked me up early the next morning. When I returned to the hotel, Marwan murmured something about not having enough time to obtain my security clearance. He said it would be easier to stay in Arafat's suite with me and watch the event on TV. I didn't understand why he didn't want to go to the White House, but things were going so well, I didn't question it. I was enjoying Marwan, and it felt as though our months of separation hadn't happened. We settled into cozy chairs in front of a large-screen TV with some aides. It was a sunny morning, the windows were open, and a comfortable breeze filled the room. Tuning the TV to CNN, we saw many familiar faces taking their seats, friends stopping to greet one another with smiles and nods.

Suddenly the bottom left-hand corner of the TV screen was squared off, and Suha Arafat's face appeared. A CNN reporter announced that live prearranged coverage of Mrs. Arafat watching this historic event would be taking place from her home in Tunis. It took a moment to realize what was going on—and to realize that *no one* in the room had expected this coverage of Suha. The men looked stunned, and Marwan cursed at the TV. Two great victories were taking place on the screen—one political, the other personal. In a bold move, Suha Arafat had found a way to be included.

She was shown on a split screen throughout the entire event. She even wept as Arafat and Israel's foreign minister, Shimon Peres, shook hands, and her reactions quickly became the focus of the commentary. I couldn't wait to see how Arafat's entourage would react to this triumph. After the signing, I could hear the motorcade pull up to the hotel and chatter on walkie-talkies that Arafat was heading straight back to the suite and didn't want to speak to the crowds of reporters. The media in front of the hotel and on his floor were told that a press conference would be arranged later. Questions would have to wait.

I planned to melt into the background and take my cues from

Marwan. The door of the suite swung open, and Arafat walked in, motioning for it to be shut. I sensed that he needed a few moments to contemplate the impact of this historic event. He stood there looking at us, frozen and tearful. Arafat knew that his opposition would use his signing the agreement as a weapon against him if it failed. Not used to seeing his leader in such a vulnerable mood, Marwan turned to me and ordered me to hug him. I walked to Arafat and told him he made many people very proud and that I sincerely hoped that he and the people in the Middle East, both Palestinians and Israelis, would see the benefits of this historic day.

Several aides bustled in, shouting about Suha's impromptu appearance on TV. Arafat looked surprised. Before he could respond, a wave of photographers and journalists who had been waiting in the hallway crowded into the room. Arafat wanted his first picture to be with Marwan and me. In the background, I could hear Arafat's aides brooding about Suha's new-found stardom. Suha's beaming brother and sister then appeared. Other guests would bring it up quietly, not sure if they should acknowledge what had happened or pretend they never saw it. A car was then sent to bring Deena and Tarik to join us for the afternoon.

That evening, the roster of guests who came to congratulate Arafat was historic in itself. Among them were former President Jimmy Carter and the Reverend Jesse Jackson. I was struck by the palpable warmth between Jewish and Palestinian leaders in that suite, and the evening was full of excitement. Meanwhile, Marwan and I had fallen into a familiar pattern, greeting friends, running around as though we had never separated. He was charming, and it was seductive to me.

Very late that evening, exhausted by the day's events, I sat alone in Arafat's suite. My children were back at home, the Secret Service was stationed in the hallway, and Marwan was in a meeting. I heard the click of Arafat's bedroom door. He strolled out of his room wearing a gray jogging outfit and slippers, *sans* headdress. I recalled that my mother (who disliked Arafat simply because of his attire) had given that jogging suit to my husband as a present. Arafat had seen Marwan unpack it and admired it, so Marwan gave it to him. If only my mother knew! He and I sat on the couch together while he ate an apple. I told him how Suha's presence on TV made the event more human. He didn't comment, but he smiled contentedly.

The next day began early, with friends from the community asking Marwan if he could arrange for them to come and congratulate Arafat. Our dear friend Sami, who had suffered from polio as a child and walked with a leg brace, came to meet him. They sat on sofas across from each other, and when a photographer asked if they wanted a snapshot together, Arafat, sensitive to Sami's handicap, jumped off the couch to sit next to him. When my six-year-old son wandered in with a small bag of chips, Arafat chased him around the room for the bag, teasing and tickling him along the way. Tarik later accompanied his dad and Arafat to a TV station for an interview. During the station break, Arafat wanted Tarik to sit in his place as a joke. Marwan didn't allow it, but these little windows into Arafat's character were telling. He was loved by some, reviled by others—but in those days, I was able to see him as simply human.

That evening, Marwan and I went to an elegant dinner at the Egyptian ambassador's house. I was falling for Marwan all over again. Maybe now that he was so happy with his work, he would be less focused on monitoring my activities. Maybe, I thought, now that the Palestinians had reached this milestone, he would be free to expand his world a bit. I didn't want this visit to end. I tried to broach the subject of our marriage, but he brushed me off: "We'll talk about it later."

The following day, the entourage left as quickly as it had arrived. As a congratulatory gesture, the king of Morocco had sent his personal 747 to take the delegation to China, their next stop. Jesse Jackson insisted that Arafat stop at his home for lunch before taking off. Arafat hung out of the limousine window, waving to crowds in the Washington streets, en route to Jackson's house (this to the dismay of the Secret Service, who had gone to the trouble of making a mannequin that looked like Arafat and placing it in another car to divert any possible assassination attempts). Arafat was basking in his image as a peacemaker.

I also made the trip to Andrews Air Force Base in a motorcade that included various diplomats as well as Suha's family. When we arrived, we mingled at a small reception given by the Palestinian mission, attended by the Arab ambassadors and their wives as well as various others who had been instrumental in the peace signing. It was exhilarating to be there, knowing we were witnessing history as it unfolded. I couldn't help but feel happy about the future. The press was waiting near the plane in a roped-off area, each with a small travel bag in the hopes of being chosen to go on the China trip. At some point, Marwan would walk over to them and handpick ten journalists out of the hundred or so who had gathered. The stories that would be available to them on this journey could potentially make their careers. I knew that I, like most of them, would be left behind.

As the reception ended, with Marwan distracted by the press, I was directed to the red carpet leading to the plane. Arafat walked down the carpet with my husband behind him, hugging everyone goodbye. I didn't want to be in this official ceremony. I needed to tell my husband that I wanted to be on that plane. In an exchange that lasted less than a minute, I told him this, but he refused, citing concerns about my leaving the children with my mother and their nanny. He said it was not time for a conversation; he had to keep walking. In nearly eleven years of marriage, there never seemed to be an appropriate time for a conversation. Then he headed up the stairs onto the plane, back into his world.

After he left, we spoke several times by phone. I said I wanted us to have time together to reevaluate our marriage, but it was difficult to get Marwan to speak in anything but superficial terms. Finally we agreed to meet in Europe six weeks later, during Thanksgiving. Adnan Khashoggi, the Saudi billionaire who had made his fortune as an international power broker, was friends with Marwan and would be our host. They traveled in the same circles in Europe, but we'd never met. Around this time, Marwan was working on facilitating joint projects between the Palestinians and Israelis for infrastructure, telecommunications, and utilities. This economic cooperation was a condition of the DOP. Marwan often represented the government's interest on behalf of Arafat. Adnan was advising him on these agreements.

I arrived at Adnan's home in Paris a few hours before Marwan got there. He lived in a six-story limestone house on the exclusive Sixteenth Arrondissement, a neighborhood that was often said to be full of deposed leaders, although I had no idea which ones. Adnan greeted me warmly, asking if I would mind waiting in the sitting room off his bedroom, the only area unoccupied by people waiting to do business with him. His butler served me tea; then his wife, a niece of the former shah of Iran, came in to introduce herself. She was a striking young woman, very tall with short black hair. They had been married a few years and had two toddlers. Sometimes the house became so crowded, she told me, that they had to remove their children from their rooms and direct the overflow to wait in the children's nursery.

When Marwan arrived, he seemed happy to see me but maintained a certain reserve. Still, he invited me to sit in on several meetings with people from various parts of the world eager to take advantage of new business opportunities made possible by the peace agreement. Palestine would need to be built from scratch. I was amazed by the fact that most of these people had never before even recognized Palestine. Now everyone was a friend, each wanting a piece of the pie while building it into a prosperous country. A committee had been set up to coordinate economic assistance, spearheaded by Norway. But funds were slow to come, because the donor countries (which included the United States, Japan, Russia, and Canada) found no acceptable infrastructure and accountability to channel their contributions. It was essential for the Palestinian leadership to show some visible evidence of an improvement in daily life in order to keep a momentum of support. These meetings with private investors were critical.

The final meeting that evening was with an Israeli businessman who had come to discuss the future of some of the utilities that would be built in the West Bank. Under occupation, the Israelis had controlled all the utilities in Palestine. Marwan signed off on an agreement with him, though it was clear that the man would benefit. "I am doing this for my country, not because I like you," Marwan said flatly. I didn't know the details, but it was evident Marwan felt his side was being exploited. The man was silent. To break the ice, I tried to jump into the conversation with small talk. I discovered that he had lived in Washington, D.C., before we did and that we had actually lived in the same apartment—we had moved in after he had moved out. I thought this was a humorous coincidence. Marwan wasn't quite so amused.

At last, Adnan called, letting us know that it was time for dinner. I was tired and hoped we were going someplace nearby. Several Rolls Royces were waiting for us. Adnan's assistant came out and got into one car, and some of his staff piled into another. Marwan and I slid into a car with Adnan and his wife. Adnan instructed the driver to take us to the airport, because he had made a dinner reservation in London. What else could I do? I went along as if it were a perfectly ordinary occurrence. We flew on his plane, a 737 appointed with a lounge, a bedroom, and more hors d'oeuvres than anyone could possibly eat on such a short flight.

In London we were greeted by Adnan's cars and staff and taken to a private dining room at the Dorchester Hotel. A prominent Israeli businessman happened to be in the restaurant and came over to introduce himself. He was invited to sit down. They shared ideas, and Marwan used the opportunity to tell him he thought an airport needed to be built in the Gaza Strip. The Israeli couldn't understand why this was important. They needed basic infrastructure: roads, sewer systems, phone lines. Why start with a luxury like an airport? Marwan explained that it was for the self-esteem of the people. Everywhere they went, they had been met with suspicion, resistance, and humiliation. Now they could have their own airport, allowing them to come and go freely. The men never came to an agreement, but conversations that seemed unthinkable in the past were actually happening. The seeds of hope had been planted.

We walked through London the next day, shopping. Marwan was even willing to go to the Tate Gallery with me and look at paintings. But I still felt a coolness I hadn't detected in Washington. Standing in Adnan's living room the evening before my departure, Marwan instructed me: "Go home tomorrow and get the children. I will meet you back here for ten days next month at Christmastime." That was all. I had no idea what he had in mind.

The children, then six and eight, arrived with me back in Paris in December, and we settled into a beautiful hotel suite near the

Champs Elysées. Marwan came in from Tunisia. It felt wonderful to have my family together again. The kids were excited to see him. I ordered a Christmas tree for the suite and decorated it. Marwan appeared distracted. Our social life was as full as ever, and there was little time for deep conversation. We had several friends arriving in Paris for the holidays. We stayed busy, having nice lunches and dinners with them, taking the children to Versailles and other historical sites. My daughter was fascinated with Marie Antoinette's jail cell, and so was I. The doomed queen had dressed every day in her finery, sat behind her beautiful caged writing desk, and waited to be executed.

Meanwhile, Marwan had been receiving phone calls at the suite from an American woman in Tunis. Marwan told me it was the same woman who had hosted him and our children at her villa the previous summer. He said he was doing business with her husband. On Christmas morning, the phone rang, and I answered because Marwan had gone downstairs. It was she. Marwan had just phoned her from the lobby, so she knew he wasn't in the room. She told me they were seeing each other in Tunis, and she wanted to know if he and I were reconciling, because he wouldn't tell her.

They had met, she told me, the previous spring. "I thought you were married!" I blurted, stunned. She told me that she and her husband had split up, because of Marwan. She thought Marwan had seemed different since he returned to Tunis after the peace signing, and she wanted to know why. Suddenly, I realized why Marwan didn't want us to go to the White House: he knew we would have been seen together on TV.

She told me that her former husband was visiting her and her two children for Christmas, which had apparently upset Marwan—odd since she had no idea that Marwan and I had met in Paris over Thanksgiving. I wondered if this family holiday of ours was anything more than an orchestration to make her jealous. I didn't want to ruin Christmas for the children, so when Marwan returned from the lobby, I didn't say a word. Shaken, I continued with our previous plans to visit friends, pretending nothing had happened. Later that evening, I told him about the phone call after the children were asleep in their rooms. He denied any involvement with her, but I didn't believe him. I rationalized that we had been separated and that I had wanted the separation. But when the possibility of reconciliation emerged, I was kept in the dark about this other life of his in Tunis. I felt that once again I had trusted Marwan to treat me in a respectful way, only to be greatly disappointed. No matter what he told me, he was going back to Tunis, and I would have no way of knowing if he was involved with her.

Quietly devastated, I left Paris for Washington several days later with the children. The air was freezing when we climbed into the car waiting to take us to Charles de Gaulle Airport. It was a chill that stayed with me the rest of the winter. I remained secluded with my children and reflected on the last twelve years of my life. Occasionally the woman would call from Tunis and tell me she was still seeing Marwan. Then he would call and deny it. One day I called Marwan at his home, and his driver answered and told me he wasn't there. Marwan phoned back about an hour later, saying he had been in a meeting. The woman called me the next day and said she was at Marwan's home when I called and that he had told the driver to say he wasn't there. "I feel so sorry for you," she told me. "He treats you terribly."

The situation was wearing on me. I knew if I packed up my children and headed to Tunis, there was a chance we could resume our relationship. But I had to ask myself if I really wanted this in the long run. I'd been entranced once again by the man I saw at the peace signing, my husband, the father of my children. I began to reach out to old friends. I had several phone conversations with a college friend in New York, and she helped me see that what I needed was self-confidence, enough to believe that this wasn't the right kind of relationship for me. It was true: my confidence had been chipped away by years of designing my life around someone else's.

Marwan and I had been speaking from time to time on the phone, and he continued to call daily to speak with the children. I stopped trying to reinvent our relationship. I knew what was coming: divorce. At the very least, I wanted it to be amicable. Marwan returned to Washington in the spring of 1994 with Arafat, seeking the funds that donor countries had committed to Palestine's reconstruction. (The Palestinians wanted to monitor these funds themselves. Other countries wanted the funds to flow through an international committee. The Palestinians therefore thought that they were being accused of being incapable of governing themselves.) This time, Suha came along on the trip. I went to the hotel to meet her and to see Marwan. There was security everywhere, but nowhere near the kind of fanfare that accompanied the previous visit. I was met downstairs by an aide and taken to Arafat's suite. Marwan answered the door, and I walked into an informal meeting of Arab foreign ministers. As introductions were being made, Mrs. Arafat, whom I had still not met, burst in from an adjoining bedroom and exclaimed, "Debbie, you are the most courageous woman in the world! You are married to the most difficult man I know!" Her impromptu statement in front of these men shocked me and them. I went into the bedroom to see the Arafats' new baby. Suha complained to me that Arafat listened to Marwan more than he listened to her. I could relate.

Marwan and I were formal with each other but friendly. My cousin Donna Shalala was in President Clinton's cabinet, serving as secretary of health and human services at the time. I called and let her know Marwan was in town and wanted to see her. We went together to her office. We chatted over tea as Marwan enumerated the many needs of the Palestinian people and how urgently they needed funds. Donna explained that accountability was crucial. "I oversee the largest budgets in the U.S. government, and I have to account for every penny that is spent," she said. Marwan understood. He had a simple request: he asked for pencils. Students in Palestine had nothing to write with, so they could not do their work. Donna looked surprised, and at that moment, I think we all realized how much we take for granted. She promised to send the pencils.

There was a reception that evening with Prime Minister Rabin of Israel and Arafat. They stood behind their podiums on the small stage in front of an intimate group of seventy people. They joked and smiled at each other. There was no question in my mind that they were committed to a common vision of peace.

Marwan came the next afternoon to take the children out. He told me he had seen a lawyer that morning to proceed with our divorce. "I cannot change, and you have lost your tolerance," he said. It was over. I cried on and off for the next few days, even when we went together to see the lawyer. It was finally time to let go.

CHAPTER SIX

Mrs. Arafat

IN THE SUMMER OF 1995, I MOVED WITH MY CHILDREN
to Newport Beach, California, where my father and brothers
lived. My father was thrilled to have his grandchildren and only
daughter nearby, but he decreed that the children call him by his
first name, George, and not refer to him as their grandfather. He
insisted that I not embarrass him by asking Marwan for support,
quickly resuming his role as patriarch. Newport was a sunny, ster-
ile environment of manicured lawns, surfers, and a Mercedes dealership the size of a Mormon temple. It was quiet, and the people
I met, especially the teenagers, seemed fairly removed from world
events—so different from where I'd just come from.

I was looking at different business options for myself, even pursuing several ideas that Adnan and I had discussed together after our meeting in Paris. Marwan had been going back and forth between the Gaza Strip and Ramallah, having returned triumphantly with Arafat in 1994 after the peace signing. Two hundred thousand people had swarmed the streets to greet Arafat. My family and I had watched news footage of Arafat with Marwan at his side, and we cheered them on. Marwan was working around the clock to implement the DOP. He was planning to run for the Palestinian Legislative Council (Parliament) office in the first Palestinian elections, representing Gaza City.

The children spoke with Marwan on the phone often. I was determined that they wouldn't be affected by the divorce. I explained that we were still together as far as their lives were concerned. Since he had traveled so often while we were married, his absence didn't feel unusual. I began to reflect on how much I'd changed since the beginning of my marriage. For once I was looking forward to an independent future, one where I pursued my own dreams instead of only supporting someone else's. I thought of the women I had met when I was with Marwan, women who were carving a place for themselves in the world I'd just left. They, like me, would have been rendered invisible if it were up to the men who surrounded them: Raymonda Tawil, Suha Arafat, Queen Dina, and many others. I wondered if they would be willing to let me record their stories.

I decided to test the waters by calling Suha Arafat. I dialed her number in the Gaza Strip, miles away from the bikini-dotted beaches and Mercedes dealerships of California. A testy guard answered the phone. When I asked if Suha was there, he abruptly said no and hung up. I tried again, this time mentioning my name. He immediately changed his tone, and Suha came on the phone, clearly excited to speak with me.

I assumed her situation hadn't changed much and that she

remained an outsider among Arafat's inner circle. She wanted to know how quickly I could come see her. She wanted to talk. She told me that my husband had "secretly" taken another wife, the same woman he'd been seeing in Tunis. Arafat had been the witness at their small wedding ceremony. I was surprised and wondered why he hadn't told me. But strangely, I wasn't upset. I'd been through so much already, this didn't faze me.

Before hanging up, Suha mentioned that she planned to be in Paris in a few weeks, so we decided to meet there instead of in Gaza. I would stay with her mother, Raymonda Tawil, whom I had not seen or been in touch with for several years. She was living in Paris, writing her second memoir. When I asked various people from the Middle East about some of the women they considered courageous, Raymonda's name always seemed to be the first one spoken. I had a feeling she would want to know all about my divorce when I arrived.

I left for Paris in late 1995 with the intention of staying ten days. I went directly to Raymonda's simple two-bedroom apartment, which was crammed wall-to-wall with books. As I anticipated, she had many questions, wanting to know all about my life, my children, my divorce, what I liked to read, my interests. Her phone didn't stop ringing from the moment I set foot in the house. After each call, she announced who it was. She loved to be at the hub.

We talked all day. I was accustomed to remaining passive and quiet, but here was someone who drew me out and was interested in my thoughts and ideas. That evening, her driver took us to one of her favorite cafés—one that Simone de Beauvoir, one of her heroes, had frequented. In the course of conversation, I happened to mention the bond between mothers and daughters and that Khalil Gibran, author of *The Prophet,* had written that the most beautiful word the human lips could utter was *mother.*

"You have just put your hand on my wounds," she told me, her eyes welling with tears. She began to tell me the story of her own mother, whose name was Christmas.

Christmas was a raven-haired beauty who lived in upstate New York until, as a teenager, her parents took her back to their homeland of Palestine. There she was introduced to a young man and fell in love. She missed the freedom of the United States, though, and after giving birth to Raymonda and two sons, she told her husband that she found her life unbearable and too restrictive. She asked for a divorce.

He complied but made her leave town without even giving her the chance to say goodbye to her children. He told eight-year-old Raymonda and her two brothers that their mother had died. "Perhaps he thought that a dead woman's memory was easier to live with than the humiliation of divorce," Raymonda said.

Christmas lived in a town several hours away, separated from her children and without any way to contact them. She joined the International Red Cross, hoping that if she became a volunteer in a respected organization, she could one day find a way back to the town she had been forced to leave and reunite with her children. Raymonda, meanwhile, had been sent off to boarding school and was deeply depressed by the "death" of her mother. The war between Jews and Arabs broke out in 1948, and Raymonda's father went missing. After several months, the nuns at her boarding school assumed she'd been orphaned and therefore wouldn't have money for room and board. She was moved to an orphanage affiliated with the school. They took away her nice clothes and her privileges and made her work for her board. She felt despair and intense loneliness, crying herself to sleep each night.

One day a woman from the Red Cross visited her school. She was a colleague of her mother, living in the same town, and had been sent on a volunteer mission. Christmas had asked the woman to find her daughter during her trip. After making inquiries, the woman was directed to Raymonda's boarding school. When she got there, she pulled Raymonda aside to tell her that her mother was alive and showed her a recent picture.

"Can you imagine?" Raymonda asked me. I couldn't.

The woman warned Raymonda not to tell anyone and promised her that her mother would one day return. Raymonda carried the picture everywhere with her and slept with it under her pillow. She kept the secret to herself, not even telling her brother.

One day several months later, Raymonda's father came to the school. He had been shot in the leg while fleeing Palestine during the war and had walked through the mountains to Lebanon. He underwent treatment, then returned to see his daughter. Raymonda was shocked and ecstatic: she had her father back, and the nuns returned her old privileges.

A few months after that, Christmas managed to return. When she did, she flagged down a Red Cross ambulance and demanded that the driver take her to Raymonda's boarding school. The little girl clung to her mother. They left the school to find Raymonda's brother and give him the news. Next, Christmas tracked down her former husband and confronted him. When she did, she declared that she would never leave her children again. Her husband's lie was exposed. From then on, Raymonda lived with her mother.

Christmas had worked with the Red Cross in the newly formed state of Israel in 1948, helping both Palestinians and Jews. Because of this, she was interrogated by Arabs and accused of collaborating with Israelis. Raymonda said that her mother was miraculously able to talk her way out of any situation and that she taught Raymonda to be brave and to find humanity in people.

"Is it better to die a hero or stay alive as a coward?" she asked me as we got up to leave the café. Then she casually mentioned that her apartment had been ransacked not so long ago, likely a message to Arafat from a group opposing the peace signing. I felt slightly uneasy as she continued to tell me that years before, a bomb had been planted in her car outside her home in Palestine. She had been sitting on her balcony when the car, parked on the street below, suddenly exploded.

"Who planted it?" I asked.

She told me that Israelis had come to her house the next morning and told her they thought the Arabs had done it because she had relations with the Israelis. But Raymonda told them, "No. I think you did it; it was too well done." In fact, she had debated a well-known Israeli politician on television two days before the incident.

I suggested we walk home, trying not to let on that I didn't want to get into her car. She sensed my reluctance right away and told me I wasn't the only one who was frightened. She had recently hired a driving instructor in Paris. When the young man arrived and saw who she was, he refused to give her lessons and left.

I woke up early the next morning and wandered into the kitchen. A cook was preparing lunch for a group of visitors who would be arriving later. The new director of Palestinian TV was coming with two broadcast journalists from French Channels 5 and 2 TV who had been stationed in the Middle East.

After the guests arrived and the introductions were made, everyone started to speak in Arabic. It reminded me of the isolation I'd felt when Marwan's colleagues spoke Arabic and I felt excluded from the conversation. But this time, it was different. Raymonda announced to the room, without hesitation, that my Arabic was limited so it would be better to conduct all conversations in English. This was the first time in all the years since I had met Marwan that anyone had insisted on including me in conversation. As I watched Raymonda hold court, I could imagine her twenty years earlier, with the same passion, pumping hope and ideas into a different generation of people.

Raymonda had wanted to move to Paris when her children were young and study at the Sorbonne, but she knew that if she left the family, her husband would not let her return. So here she was years later, betrayed by time, arriving to find only the ghosts of Sartre and Simone de Beauvoir in the cafés where they had long ago left their mark.

I saw the respect her guests had for her. They spoke about the magazines and journals she published, many of them displayed on tables throughout her house. She had come a long way from her days as a young bride, married to a well-off banker in Jordan. She had longed for her Palestinian homeland, although it didn't offer Jordan's freedom. When her husband had the opportunity to take his business to Palestine, she was happy to move with their four young children and try to work for peace.

It was an uphill battle. Raymonda had Israeli friends, classmates from boarding school who, like her, opposed occupation and wanted to find a peaceful solution. Maybe this was hard for others to understand. For this reason, many Arabs considered her a traitor. Once, while crossing Jordan's border, she was taken into custody by the Jordanians and driven to a deserted spot high in the mountains. Although she was interrogated about her "collaborations" with the Israeli enemies, she was released, and she returned to Israel. There she was placed under arrest by the Israelis for collaborating with the PLO. No one could figure out if she was a friend or a threat. They were unaccustomed to dealing with someone who could see both sides of this political conflict.

Living in occupied territory, she thought nothing of risking her life to violate the occupation-imposed curfew if someone was in need of medical care. Often, sick people called her or simply showed up at her house. She tied a white cloth on her car—a sign of peace—and drove them to the hospital. One day she wanted to transport a sick baby to a blood bank and asked her husband to come along. He refused, fearing that they could be shot for violating occupation rules. "At that moment," she told me, "I decided to make a revolution against my husband."

She took their car out herself, baby by her side, and drove to a friend's house. She stood outside her window with the baby in her arms and yelled for her friend to come down, to show her support. "Put down your books!" she cried. "Freedom begins by coming down to the street now! This is where your doctrine lives!" Sure enough, her friend came down, and together they took the child to safety.

Raymonda was used to these kinds of risks and wasn't afraid of being a target. Her journalistic reports of life under occupation, which she sent to various news agencies, caused the Israelis to put her under house arrest, restricting her communication with others for long stretches of time. When she did find a way to leak stories about the occupation, she woke up to soldiers in her home and told her children not to cry as she was carried off to jail.

It was during one of her house arrests that she decided to "look at all my prisons, all my walls." Her husband didn't want her to walk in the streets and have meetings in the cafés. Yearning for escape was no longer enough; she knew she had to act. Raymonda began writing about her life and eventually published a book in 1979, *My Home, My Prison,* about life under all forms of occupation, personal and political. It was highly popular in Israel and made waves in twenty-six other countries. It was around this time that she founded the Palestinian press service in Jerusalem. Seeing the reverence with which her peers now treated her, it was obvious her work had had an impact.

One of the downsides to her activist lifestyle was the loss of frequent contact with her family. Once a year, the Israelis gave Christmas permission to meet Raymonda at a fence separating Jordan and the West Bank. Communication outside of meeting on this designated day was not possible due to the occupation. Then one year Raymonda traveled to the fence to see her mother. She waited all day, but her mother never arrived. Raymonda learned several days later that her mother had died two weeks earlier. It was the second time she'd lost her mother, this time for good. But she continued to follow in her footsteps, and her daughter Suha did the same.

Suha, who arrived in Paris the following day, called me from a friend's apartment and suggested that I come over later in the evening, after her daughter, Zahwa, was in bed. She was planning to tell me all about the PLO over pizza. When my taxi pulled up to the turn-of-the-century building on the Left Bank, several police cars were stationed outside. I entered a small, dimly lit lobby and was confronted by four French policemen with machine guns, their menacing silhouettes reflected on the cement walls. After calling Suha, they allowed me to ride the elevator up into her cloistered world.

I could hear her high-pitched greetings before she even opened the door. The apartment was simple and spare, with a few large rooms and scant furnishings. Her friend was no longer living there and had left only a few necessities for the occasional guest. Suha was staying there with her daughter and her British assistant, Susie, who also served as the baby's nanny. She led me into a room where she stored artifacts from her recently completed trip to Africa. She told me that she and the "president," as Arafat was formally addressed, were almost always in different parts of the world and rarely traveled together. I knew all too well that this pleased her husband's entourage. As we sank into an overstuffed sofa, I broached this subject. Suha's enthusiasm waned. Her breathing became uneven.

"You can't imagine the stress given to one person," she said. "I've developed heart palpitations now."

It all began in 1985 when she had met Yasir Arafat in Jordan. She was twenty-one years old, and he was fifty-one. She had been living in Paris and attending the Sorbonne, her mother's dream. She was invited by her parents to accompany them on a visit to meet Arafat in Jordan. Years before that, growing up under occupation, she associated his name with the revolution, a name synonymous with hope and freedom. She, like other Palestinians, believed that he would lead them away from a life under occupation. In her preteen years, she had demonstrated at her school in Palestine, marching with Arafat's picture in her hands—and was suspended from classes as punishment. She said Raymonda had encouraged it. When Suha and Arafat finally met, she saluted him.

I asked her what it was like growing up with Raymonda.

"Growing up, going to school, seeing armies, demonstrators, gunfire, afraid to walk in the streets, in a house where my mother was very active—she was different from the other women—we could feel the hostility toward her," she said. "The people weren't used to an outspoken, courageous woman. You had to be much more of an adult than a child. My mother always encouraged our strength."

Perhaps that had prepared her for life with Arafat. Their relationship developed after 1985, although Suha said she had no idea that it would ever grow into what it did. It started to blossom in 1989 in Paris when she was asked to take care of his visit there, since her family were trusted friends of Arafat. He seemed interested in her and went so far as to tell her, "If I were younger, I would have married you." He began calling her often, wanting her to help him with a trip or to translate something. "He is just a human being with emotions like everyone else," Suha explained to me. He asked her to leave Paris and live in Tunis where the PLO was headquartered. Her feelings for him were growing as well, so she decided to go.

"I agreed to marry him," she said. "I was so young; I didn't understand the pain that could come with it." As she spoke, she sometimes gasped for air, as though she was unsure that the next breath would come. Arafat wanted to keep the marriage a secret. He was afraid his people would oppose it. Even now, Suha was still trying to understand why. She wondered if he was haunted by an interview he had given to journalist Oriana Fallaci thirty years earlier, in which he famously declared that he was "married to the revolution." Maybe the idea of marriage simply frightened him.

Arafat had fallen in love once before, in 1973 in Lebanon, with a young woman named Nada Yushruti. She was a PLO activist and had been married to a fellow Fatah leader who had been killed in a freak construction accident. She was said to be highly intelligent, first in her class at the American University in Beirut. At the time, the country was divided between Christians and Muslims, and civil war was breaking out.

Nada was friends with the Lebanese president, and so the PLO asked her to speak to him. Returning home from her visit with him at the presidential palace, she was killed. There were various theories regarding her death—from Israeli agents punishing Arafat, to her being caught spying while at the palace. News of Nada's death reached Arafat while he was in a meeting. "He cried like a baby," remembered Said Kamal, an adviser to Arafat, who watched in dismay as the PLO leader banged his head on the wall. According to *Arafat: In the Eyes of the Beholder*, by John Wallach, when once asked if he had been in love with her, Arafat had replied, "She was very beautiful, I was going to marry her. She had accepted, and then she was killed."

Fifteen years later, Arafat had fallen in love again. For Suha, who was used to saying whatever crossed her mind, I knew that keeping her marriage a secret must have been agonizing.

"If I did not love him," Suha told me, "I think I would have left. I had three years of marriage without anyone knowing. It was frustrating to be married to someone very important, a political figure, and not show how I felt. I was just waiting for things to be announced." Their time alone was spent under the guise of work. Their living quarters were in the same building as his office. Meanwhile, Suha knew Raymonda wouldn't approve because of the age difference and the danger. Raymonda loved him as a leader, but as the husband of her daughter—that was different.

Rumors that began circulating in Tunis that Suha was his mistress got to Raymonda as well. True to form, she decided to step in. She flew to Tunis with a female journalist friend to ask Arafat about it. They were alone in the room with him, and he kept denying the marriage. Their confrontation became heated until he finally admitted it to her and left.

"I was relieved," Suha said. "My husband and I never discussed it—events happen by themselves. All of a sudden he started saying 'yes' when he was asked if he was married."

Initially his entourage treated her more kindly because they no longer saw her as his mistress. But gradually they grew resentful. After all, he had said he was married to the revolution. Arafat wasn't very supportive. Suha felt he had married her and then said, "Face the world alone." Suha described the men around her husband as "the cheap entourage of the Palestinian revolution, cheap people treating me in a cheap way."

She thought they considered her a threat because she told Arafat what she thought about everything, and many of her positions clashed with those of his advisers. She was persuasive, and Arafat confided in her. They tried to control her, but she let them know that she made her own schedule and spoke to whomever she chose, including the media.

Our chat was suddenly interrupted by noises in the baby's room. We both rose and headed toward the nursery to investigate. Susie appeared, explaining it was only her moving about. "Don't worry, Mrs. Arafat, there are only good spirits surrounding the baby and me. I won't let anyone cross this line." She drew an imaginary line with her finger and smiled. Suha relaxed, and we returned to the living room. Being married to a moving target created an atmosphere of inescapable tension, making spontaneity a luxury of the past. Even our simple request to order pizza had been declined: there was no way that the food or the delivery people could withstand the scrutiny of her guards.

When we settled back down, I told Suha that I had been present three years earlier in Arafat's suite during the peace signing. I still didn't understand why she hadn't insisted on accompanying him and how she managed to surprise everyone with her CNN appearance. She looked me straight in the eye: "I am going to tell you what happened for the first time." She mentioned the book *Arafat: In the Eyes of the Beholder,* widely respected as an accurate account of Arafat's life. Suha said that Wallach wrote that one of the reasons that Arafat went to America for the White House peace signing was because of his wife. No one had known what he had meant by that except for a handful of people.

The U.S. government, which had maintained a strained relationship with Arafat, was not going to invite him to the United States for the peace signing. The peace treaty would be signed by Mahmoud Abbas, and Arafat would not be included. She knew that if Arafat didn't go to the United States for the peace signing, the Palestinians would never consider it legitimate. Suha secretly worked with her own contacts in Washington, trying to change this. Some in the PLO were suspicious, but no one knew what she was up to. Arafat was giving her messages to convey, and she was going back and forth between him and her contacts in the United States. They were running out of time as the signing approached. Then Suha was told by her contacts in Washington to have Arafat put his name on the list as head of the peace delegation and send it to President Clinton to see if it would be accepted. Arafat did so, and it worked. Since Arafat was now permitted to go, Prime Minister Rabin of Israel said he would also go. Having both leaders present was a huge breakthrough and a direct result of Suha's work. The people she had worked with in Washington had looked forward to having Suha there for the signing as well.

Arafat announced this turn of events to the Palestinian delegation. Shortly after, Abu Massan, one of the head negotiators (who eventually became the president of Palestine), called Suha to tell her that Arafat's advisers would be very upset if she decided to go. Suha was stunned. Arafat told her that he had taken care of their wives for years, making sure they had homes, schooling for their children, and medical care, so he was puzzled as to why they wouldn't accept her. Suha told me that Abu Massan had given Arafat an ultimatum: "I go or she goes."

"I said, 'You must go alone. I won't go. Remember, the story now is the story of the Palestinian people, not a personal story. The story is you: I only want the Palestinian issue to be there.' So I convinced him and I did not go. The most important thing for me was that there was a signing, something to help people who have been suffering for many years. It was not the time for insider quarreling."

When Suha told her American contacts what had happened, they were upset. They thought she deserved to be there. They told her not to worry, that it would be as though she *was* there. She wasn't sure what they had meant by that.

Arafat and the delegation left for Washington without her. The next day, she received an unexpected call from the president of CNN. He wanted to arrange for a crew to film her watching the peace signing from her living room in Tunis. She finally understood.

"I was shown on television more than all the ladies who were present. It was a shock for everybody. They prevented me from coming, and I was all over the press—I had more visibility than anyone. I couldn't go anyplace without people commenting. I had two months of coverage all over the world and stories only on me. It backfired. Their plan did not work. I had more publicity than if I would have gone to the signing."

"Did you tell your husband?" I had to ask. It seemed unthinkable that she wouldn't.

"No! When I do interviews or meet with the press, I don't tell him or get permission. I talk to who I want. He called me from Washington and he said, 'What's going on? Each time I look at the television, you are on it!' I just laughed."

I liked Suha's brand of warfare. She ignored everyone and did what she wanted. This frustrated the men around Arafat, of course. She told me that she had once had an audience with the pope. She traveled to Rome, and when she arrived, she was told that someone had canceled it. She found out that "someone" was one of her husband's aides. She set another appointment, informing the Vatican to ignore any subsequent cancellations unless they came directly from her. She eventually returned, without informing anyone else, and met with the pope.

Susie wandered into the living room, wrapped in a warm robe, to bring us tea. "Suha used to let herself be vulnerable. She trusted everyone and has learned the hard way. The people she thought were closest to her have betrayed her," Susie said, sitting down.

Zahwa had been born into this way of life. Suha had given birth to her in a Paris hospital, by cesarean section. Zahwa was two days old when Raymonda entered her room, followed by the police. They said she and the baby had to evacuate immediately. There was a bomb threat against the family. They took Zahwa and wrapped her little body in bulletproof materials, then wheeled Suha out while her child wailed.

Still, she had been hopeful that a new atmosphere would prevail following the landmark peace signing. She spoke passionately to me about her ongoing efforts to speak out for a democratic process in the newly formed government of Palestine, to speak out against any violation of human rights that might happen in her land. She had once heard about a family who had arranged a marriage for their nine-year-old daughter in exchange for money. She reported the story to the general prosecutor, and the mother and father were ultimately put in jail. These were her real challenges, much more important than the challenges from her husband's entourage.

As Suha told me that night, "Images don't make changes, voices and action make changes." There had been a Palestinian law that stated women had to have permission from a husband, brother, or father to get a passport. Suha called the vice minister of the interior, whose husband was the minister, and said, "Can you do me a favor and tell the minister we need this changed?" Now the law states that only a girl under the age of sixteen has to get such permission. She said, "It's a patriarchal society; man is the master of everything; the woman is told she is the weaker person and reminded of this all the time." She wasn't part of the government, but she let everyone know that she would try to influence what she didn't like, directly or indirectly. It was easy to see how she must have infuriated her husband and his entourage.

She and Arafat quarreled like other married couples. "Sometimes I quarrel with my husband because I can't accept what I see. I know I create problems for him, and he comes screaming, asking me, 'Why did you declare this, why did you make that declaration?' He will tell me, 'Don't say this, don't say that.' I don't even discuss it with him; I do what I want. He tells me I'm so stubborn," Suha laughed. "He tells me my daughter is stubborn like me, and I say, 'No she's more stubborn than me, so she's like you!' I believe he knows that there is no point in arguing."

The day after our nighttime talk, Raymonda, Suha, and I shopped in Paris. Raymonda bought Suha several new dresses to wear on official visits. The men around Arafat gave her very little financial support, and Arafat did not fight them on this. He was committed to his image as a man who lived only with necessities. She cried a lot that day. She seemed exhausted and lonely and explained to me that she couldn't help but feel hurt by the people trying to keep her away from her husband. She worried about her husband being assassinated. "I live in a land of widows," she said.

Suha caught me by surprise when she mentioned Golda Meir was an influence. "The prime minister of Israel? The enemy of the Palestinians?" I couldn't believe it. In spite of everything, Suha admired her for her courage, for doing what she thought was best for her people.

Did Suha see herself as courageous? "It comes from your experiences," she told me over lunch a few days later. "It's not something you are taught or you can inherit. If you don't have experiences that teach you courage, you will never be courageous. I have two strong personalities in my life, my mother and my husband, that make it possible for me to disappear in their shadows.

At first I think I was trying to figure out whose shadow to live in, and then I realized I didn't have to live in anyone's shadow. I could survive on my own, with my own voice and beliefs."

I was sitting alone reading in Raymonda's living room the following day when Zahwa, Arafat's daughter, walked in, taking shaky little toddler steps. Suha was resting, Raymonda was on the phone, and the security detail was in the kitchen. Zahwa and I had a moment alone. She walked alongside the coffee table, holding on with one hand. There was a hardcover book on the table titled *Arafat*, with a large picture of him on the cover. Zahwa saw the picture out of the corner of her eye. She looked down, stared at the cover for a few moments, and then leaned down and gently kissed the book.

I left Paris a week later. On the flight back to California, I listened to the interview tapes I'd made with Suha, and I reread my notes from Raymonda's stories. "We are one big family of a revolution, so it doesn't matter if some of the families had members that left and became rich, or some had education, or some are very poor—we are all the same when we are here," Suha had said of Palestine. "My biggest challenge now is to speak my mind for a democratic country. I want to put all my efforts forward. I cannot stay passive for any violation of human rights that might happen in my land. I have to make sure that my husband knows all the abuses of women in this country. There are a lot of things I feel I can be responsible for, and I will not stay passive. These are the real challenges, much more than the challenges from my husband's entourage. It's a patriarchal society. Man is the master of everything, and nobody will tell him not to do something. A woman is told she is the weaker person and reminded of this all the time."

I knew that firsthand.

CHAPTER SEVEN

Baha Kikhia

WHEN I RETURNED TO CALIFORNIA, MY FATHER SEEMED preoccupied. He had sold off his warranty companies several years back and had started buying offshore companies. He finally admitted to my brothers and me that he was mired in a legal battle over his offshore insurance companies, which were no longer permitted to operate in California. These companies were not regulated and could charge low rates, undercutting U.S. companies' premiums. A large lobbying effort had pushed the state government to forbid these companies to operate. My father didn't agree with the ruling, so he had decided to ignore the law as long as possible. When and if he were confronted, he'd fight. His company also did business in New York. He told us that a sting operation had been set up in a deli in New York City, near Wall Street. FBI agents posing as businessmen said they wanted to do business with his insurance company, which issued performance bonds. He was arrested when delivering his end of the bargain in person. He loved dramatizing the story and making jokes about the possibility of going to jail. He ended up appearing in front of a grand jury in New York, and his case was thrown out.

When similar charges were brought up against him in California, he expected another victory. The government tried to bargain with him: if he closed his companies, they'd drop the charges. But he refused to settle with the government, at the risk of his money being frozen indefinitely. He toyed with the investigators, who had set up an office in his own building to monitor him. He would buy them breakfast every morning and have it delivered to their office. Ultimately the government got enough evidence to go to trial, and they indicted him. He was surprised but brushed it off. He seemed to be enjoying the drama. He hired the best defense firm he could find and oversaw their every move, as though he were directing a film. As a lawyer himself, he knew how to maneuver. He expected his attorneys to play their roles and repeat the dialogue he had written for them. My brothers and I went to several dinners and meetings with his defense team. Most of the evening was spent listening to my father relive his glory days as an attorney. He couldn't grasp the seriousness of the charges facing him and was excited about his upcoming trial. But the rest of the family was stressed and frightened. I was visited by the FBI, as were my brothers. They were trying to get us to testify against our father. None of us wanted to be involved.

I remained loyal, helping him prepare each day. When the trial began, my family met him each morning at the courthouse and sat through hours of courtroom melodrama. When questioned, he made people on the jury laugh, sometimes making fun of the district attorney. Sometimes he insulted the judge. "You're trying to provoke me," she told him. "You're behaving this way so you can declare a mistrial." His own lawyers were just as frustrated. They argued with my father after court each day, begging him to let them do their work, but he insulted them as well. No one could reason with him.

The jury was out for two weeks. We tried to talk to him about planning for the future in case he lost, but he refused to even consider the possibility. Then one morning, I arrived at the court early with my father. We were waiting for my brothers and preparing to settle into another long day of pacing the halls when his lawyers came running down the hall announcing that the verdict was in. My brothers had yet to arrive. I would be the sole audience for this dreaded moment. The verdict: Guilty. Seconds later my brothers arrived, dazed. Then I heard the judge declare that all assets would be frozen. She said that he would be held without bail until his sentencing because she believed he had money hidden and was a flight risk because he spoke Spanish fluently, making it easier for him to flee to Mexico. At seventy years old, he was going to prison. Devastated, I walked behind his chair as two marshals waited to handcuff him. He turned and handed me his jewelry and his wallet. I watched him disappear.

My brothers and I gathered at my father's house, trying to absorb the shock in our own way. We spoke to his attorneys and tried to come up with a way to get him freed on bail. As soon as we were able to visit him, I began taking daily commutes to the horrific holding center in downtown Los Angeles where he insisted on being kept. He planned to appeal his bail and be freed. Once out, he would oversee his appeal and, he thought, be victorious. I would wait for hours until they called my number so that I could visit him for half an hour at best. He would give me instructions on putting together his appellate team, and then I'd drive home, thinking the whole way about how I could take care of my family.

In a short time, I had lost my marriage, my father, and all my financial support, which had gone to his legal defense. Marwan felt bad about my father's fate, but he told me he couldn't help me financially. As the oldest of my siblings, I felt responsible for the others. My father knew he could count on me, and he was right. I didn't know how to say no. He demanded I work on his motion for release on bail. I watched everything he had built disintegrate. He called constantly. It was impossible to look for other work; his trial was my full-time job. His bail appeal was ultimately denied, and finally he was sentenced. My brothers were away that day, so I sat in the courtroom alone and watched as they brought him in to stand in front of the judge. She announced in a clear, loud voice: "Five years—the maximum sentence." With his back to me, he threatened the judge and vowed revenge. Then he was taken away.

Summer finally came, and with the children out of school I could send them to visit their father in Ramallah. He was still Arafat's spokesman and adviser, and now an elected member of parliament. They were excited to visit their dad, and I was happy to distance them from the turmoil at home. Ultimately Marwan and I saw no other option than to keep the children with him while I dealt with my father's affairs.

It had occurred to me that I could rent a home in the Middle East. Since I had been married and divorced in the United States, I was entitled to child support—a modest amount, but enough for the children and me to be together in Ramallah. I arranged to rent the home of a friend, just outside Ramallah. I told Marwan, but he didn't respond. I don't think he believed I would actually do such a thing.

Telling my father was extremely difficult. This was a huge

decision; I'd never been able to fully extricate myself from his melodramas. I'd relied on him for everything. I spoke with Raymonda on the phone from time to time. As my comfortable life unraveled, hearing her voice meant more than she could know. I realized that seeing Suha and Raymonda prevail over their hardships was giving me the strength I needed to deal with my own.

My father had been moved to a "country club" facility about two hours north of Los Angeles. To get there, I had to drive down a winding two-lane road through mountains that were covered with breathtaking yellow wildflowers. We sat in the picnic area and talked. He was in good spirits until I told him that being with my children and making sure they had a comfortable life had to take precedence over his legal woes. He was upset, but he understood as a parent that I missed my children, as he now missed his. "You need to be with your children," he told me. We were finally talking, parent to parent, as equals. We both cried. Then it was my turn to leave.

I thought it would be a good change of pace to explore a new part of the world with my children. I wanted to talk more with the other women I'd known during my marriage, like Queen Dina. I was also interested in speaking with my friend Baha, who was now living just outside Washington, D.C. I decided to stop and see her on my way to the Middle East. I'd seen her on TV more often than I had seen her in person over the past few years. She appeared on countless news programs, sending pleas for the release of her husband, Mansour Kikhia, who had been the Libyan ambassador to the United Nations. He had been kidnapped while attending a human rights conference in 1993. Now, four years later, he was still missing.

I'd first met them through Marwan in 1982 in New York, when they'd been married for three years. We had gone to their modest apartment in Lower Manhattan for dinner. She was busy with guests when we arrived, but I watched her, sweeping through the room, stopping just long enough to say something clever and leave everyone laughing. She was tall and thin with dark eyes made more intense by the straight black bangs that cut across her forehead, offsetting her high cheekbones. An artist, she had a dramatic nature and a sense of mystery that matched her paintings. They hung on the walls behind her, framing her when she stopped to chat. Mansour seemed kind, gentle, and uncomplicated. He leaned against a wall most of the evening, speaking in whispers to the various other ambassadors who were attending their party.

Once the foreign minister of Libya and the Libyan ambassador to the United Nations, Mansour had resigned from his post as ambassador in 1980 and defected to the United States. When I saw him, he was in the throes of forming a human rights organization in protest of Muammar Gadhafi's policies. Social gatherings such as these were safe places for him to communicate his plans to other members of the diplomatic community.

Shortly after the U.N. resignation, he and his wife moved to Paris and in December 1983 became founding members of the Arab Organization for Human Rights (AOHR). After a ten-year span of working in exile to change Libya's policies, in 1993 Mansour traveled to Cairo to speak at an AOHR convention. It was there that he disappeared. Baha's relentless search led her to confrontations with the CIA, the Egyptian secret police, and even Gadhafi himself. Baha and I had been in regular touch since my divorce, and her first husband and Marwan had also been close friends.

When I arrived in Washington, Baha was preparing Arabic coffee for my visit. She led me into the house and paused in front of a life-size photo of her husband, standing about six feet tall. He is smiling in the portrait, with a bird of paradise hovering behind him. "He looks good," she said, as if he were really there. Then she turned to look out the window to where her son was outside playing with other neighborhood kids. Her tone changed to wistful. "He can't concentrate," she told me. "He misses his father."

Baha had had a similar experience as a child while growing up in Syria. She was twelve, the same age as her son, when her father was imprisoned. He had served in the Syrian Army in Iraq and was an adviser to King Faisal II, as his country fought their British occupiers. "He was gallant." Baha beamed. "He led the other men." When he returned home, the British soldiers imprisoned him. They built a jail just for him, where he was kept for five years. Every week, she and her mother cooked food and brought it to him when they visited.

She went to school fearing that his name would come up in her classroom, that he would be perceived as a traitor by the British supporters. When her classmates spoke of their fathers, Baha would clench her fists to keep from crying: "When you cry you are weak; you are finished," she told me. Her mother was her role model during those years. Unfailingly stoic, she just kept going, and she kept the family together.

Eventually President Abdul Nasser of Egypt helped get her father released from prison, and her family went to live in Cairo, where he was in good political standing. She never felt that she belonged in the Middle East; she was depressed and lethargic and slept as much as she could. Her family allowed her to come to New York when she was seventeen and stay with relatives. There she started selling her paintings in Greenwich Village, expressionistic pieces with broad strokes and bright colors. "You're not afraid of color," I'd once joked to her. She looked me dead in the eyes and replied: "I'm not afraid of anything."

Perched on her leopard print sofa, sipping coffee, Baha and I chatted briefly about our previous marriages. Her former husband, Hadi Toron, was an artist and diplomat from Syria who was living in New York and working at the United Nations. They had two children, but Hadi wasn't a family man. He and Marwan enjoyed going out and carousing. Eventually she got fed up. She decided to stay in America and raise her children there. "New York made me strong and I loved the freedom. I stayed alone for six years, raising my children. My art was my closest companion until I met Mansour."

Mansour, like Gadhafi, had been born in Libya while it was controlled by Italy's fascist government. Warfare was a natural part of their childhoods, as they witnessed the transference of power from one foreign occupier to another. Both men grew up envisioning a powerful, unified Arab world that would encompass all of North Africa. It would be strong enough to prevent another foreign power from ever stepping foot on their soil again.

Gadhafi attended the Royal Army School outside London. He diligently wore his Arab clothing, attracting constant attention, to demonstrate his Arab nationalism. By the time he had finished his education and returned to Libya, a U.N. decree had allowed the country to become an independent nation under the rule of their king, Idris. Gadhafi served in the king's army, rising to the rank of major. He and his fellow officers, although pleased they were no longer under foreign occupation, still believed that a stronger position for Arab unity was necessary. The nation's earnings were skyrocketing from the discovery of oil. Foreign countries would be highly motivated to invade. In September 1969, King Idris was deposed in a bloodless military coup led by Gadhafi. A revolutionary command council (RCC) was formed to rule Libya. Mansour, who had studied law at the Sorbonne, was living in France. He was called to Libya to serve as Gadhafi's new foreign minister. Their motto was "Freedom, Socialism, and Unity." In

1969, they formed a civilian cabinet to assist the RCC in implementing a democratic government. Over the years it became clearer that the proposed democratic government was becoming a dictatorship run by Gadhafi. Tension between the men grew. Mansour was agreeable on the surface and served in high-profile positions as ambassador to France and then ambassador to the United Nations while maintaining his position as foreign minister. In 1976, Gadhafi had tightened his policies against any opposition, stating that his government "has only unconditional soldiers or natural enemies." A wave of assassinations and mass arrests took place among the ranks of intellectuals and students. In March 1980, the execution of attorneys Amer Al Dughais and Mohammed Himmy, Mansour's two close friends, finally convinced him that his government would never support the ideals of democracy that he and his colleagues had fought to establish. Baha met Mansour as he was contemplating the difficult decision to resign from Gadhafi's government.

"My children were at the United Nations School, so sometimes I attended diplomatic receptions, and I was exhibiting my artwork there." She smiled at the memory. She and Mansour crossed paths many times. Eventually they were seated next to each other at a wedding reception and had the chance to speak. As he was leaving, he gave her his number. I looked at him and asked why I should call him. 'So I can invite you to dinner!' I told him that I had two children and would agree to meet only when they were at school. No dinner, just lunch. He said that was fine and wanted to know where I wanted to eat. I said, 'Burger King!'" Baha laughed again. She knew that she had managed to shock him. Being an ambassador, he was used to eating at the best restaurants in New York—but she wanted to go to Burger King because it was next to her children's school, and she didn't want to worry about being late to pick them up.

She liked that he was easygoing, though she admitted to being a bit tough on him when they started dating. After a few more meetings, she agreed to have dinner with him. At the restaurant, he asked her if she would marry him. She suggested he think about the fact that she had two young daughters who would always come first. He would always be number three, she told him, and if there were more children, he would keep going down in number, "But I told him, 'Number three is good.' He used to say, 'My God, the way you speak, you're so honest. Another man would be scared, would run away, but I like what you are saying. It makes me want you more.'" I couldn't imagine talking that way to Marwan.

Mansour respected her strong instincts to protect her children and knew that this quality was essential in a partner. At any time, he could be the target of an opposition or fanatical group. She understood his political position. She supported his resignation from his government. They married and moved to France, where they lived in a small town outside Paris. They were very happy for the next few years there. They had two more children, and Mansour used his time to advocate for human rights in Libya and throughout the Middle East. He still hoped for peaceful negotiations with Gadhafi about freeing political prisoners, freedom of speech, and implementing human rights and democratic process in Libya.

In 1992, Mansour signed an understanding of cooperation with M. Mugaryaf, the secretary general of the Libyan National Salvation Front, a coalition group representing all of the Libyan opposition groups in exile. Their goal was to convince Libya to recognize the opposition party and negotiate with it on equal footing about the future of the country. This made Mansour a leader of utmost importance within the ranks of the opposition. He had increasing political power, the reason for the continuous comings and goings of Libyan emissaries, sent by Gadhafi, to convince Mansour to put an end to his political activities and return to Libya. On October 7, 1993, Mansour, along with M. Mugaryaf, paid a visit to see his friend, Algerian president Al-Alkafi. This further infuriated the Libyan government. They feared that other Arab countries would start to isolate themselves due to Mansour's efforts.

In 1993, the third annual conference of the Arab Organization for Human Rights was to be held in Cairo. Mansour would be a key participant as one of the founding members. A sudden wave of mysterious phone calls started coming to Baha and Mansour's home in Paris. Gadhafi continued sending messengers to them, saying he wanted to talk. Then he sent the prime minister of Libya, followed by at least six more people. Mansour met with them, Baha said. He never refused. Gadhafi wanted Mansour to come back; he told Mansour through the messengers that "his people missed him and his country missed him." Mansour replied that he loved his country, but he had conditions. Number one: to accept the opposition parties so they could speak with the government. Number two: to free the political prisoners. Number three: to make the laws fair. After that, Mansour would discuss anything. He used to say to Baha, "Gadhafi is never my enemy. I don't like this word. He is our opposition and he is our leader. I want to work together. We have to correct things in a logical way."

Before his departure from Paris to the conference in Cairo, the Egyptians refused to give him his visa. Baha didn't know why, and she tried to discourage him from going. "I told him, 'Who are the Egyptians to refuse you? Don't ever forget that you were a foreign minister. Don't go to Cairo—if I were you I wouldn't go.'" He explained that the relationship between Egypt and Libya was fragile. Gadhafi employed more than 1 million Egyptians. Egypt had to be careful not to do something that would damage relations with Libya. Then one day, they suddenly decided to give him his visa. "I think it was planned," she said. The Egyptians knew he might be in danger. She thought they were trying to protect him.

It was November 29, 1993, when he left Paris for Cairo. He planned to return on December 11. After that, he was going to resign and leave things to a new generation. He called her the day after he arrived and said that he had been detained at the airport. After that, he called sporadically, usually late at night, to tell her what he'd bought for her and the kids. On December 11, she cooked dinner for the family and waited for him to arrive home. Finally his brother called her and said not to wait for him, that Mansour had sent a message saying he wasn't coming. Baha didn't panic, but she asked to see a copy of the message. She wanted to see the handwriting. When she didn't get a copy of the message the next day, she knew it was a lie. After two days of silence, she knew something was drastically wrong.

No one could locate him. She received phone calls from people in Cairo telling her not to worry, that they would find him. Then the press started calling her: the Arabic newspapers, the *New York Times*, the *Washington Post*, using the words "kidnapping, missing." "I just kept saying I had no idea, I've had no contact with him since the night before he was supposed to return to Paris," she said. "The children were told the truth. The truth is always much easier in the long run." She took them to London to see her mother and sister. Her mother encouraged her to be strong, not to worry, to take care of her family first.

After ten days, she received a phone call from a special envoy on behalf of President Hosni Mubarak of Egypt. He told her she was welcome to Egypt if she wanted to talk to officials about the disappearance. He said that their ambassador in Paris would meet her when she returned there and would organize everything. So she flew to Egypt to see what she could find out about her husband's disappearance. When she arrived, she was met by an Egyptian delegation. Behind them was a large sign at the airport that read, "Enter peacefully, you are in a peaceful place." "I told the guards, 'You should remove that sign—it is a joke? Why wasn't my husband protected?'"

The delegation led her to a room where she was met by President Mubarak's envoy. He asked her when she would like to see President Mubarak. She told him that she didn't want to see the president; she wanted to see the head of the secret police. A few days before her arrival, President Mubarak, obviously afraid of financial repercussions from Libya, had said in an interview, "Who's Mansour? Is he Syrian? I can't protect millions of people that come here." Baha asked his envoy, "Why should I go and meet with him? If he didn't recognize the problem with my husband, then why should I see him? I'm Syrian, an artist, a mother, so what does he want from me?" In front of the airport were a limousine and two Mercedes full of guards hanging out the windows with tommy guns. "I knew the cars were for me, but I made believe they weren't. I started walking in a different direction. They yelled, 'Wait, these cars are for you!' I acted shocked. I said, 'What? This is for me? It should be for my husband. I am just an artist and a mother. *This* is how you should have protected my husband!' The entire scene felt like a mockery."

Since Baha is an American citizen, the American ambassador in Egypt called her when she arrived at the hotel to see if she was all right, and she kept the U.S. embassy abreast of her whereabouts.

She contacted Dr. El-Baz of the secret police. She knew he had just met with Gadhafi. He invited her to his office the next day. With a sympathetic tone, he told her he had been with Mansour at Cairo University many years ago, that they were friends. Before he could speak further, Baha interrupted him: "Please Dr. El-Baz, tell me 'yes or no.' Do you know where my husband is?" He didn't answer. Dr. El-Baz told her he had met Gadhafi in Tripoli a few days earlier, and Gadhafi had told him that he didn't know what had happened to Mansour. "I didn't believe him," she said. "And I wasn't afraid to let him know. I told him, 'Okay, Dr. El-Baz, when you find out, let me know. Your secret service is excellent; they know where the flies fly. He was kidnapped from here, so let's start here. How did he disappear?' He just stared at me."

Guards escorted her to Mansour's room so she could collect his things. "I couldn't cry, but I was shivering from the inside out. My skin was freezing and blue." Mansour was diabetic, and she saw his insulin laid out just the way he laid it out at home. She saw his slippers at the side of the bed. Then she finally knew: he had been kidnapped. According to the hotel staff, a guest had come to see him the night before he vanished. They had coffee and soda, then Mansour walked out the door with him. Their account was vague, only that the man had an Egyptian accent. He could have been anyone.

Baha returned to Paris, and the Egyptians started an investigation. It was in the hands of the secret police, which meant they could start or stop at any time. It wasn't in the hands of the court. Among the suspects were the opposition to Gadhafi, who didn't think Mansour was aggressive enough; and Muslim fundamentalists, because Mansour didn't believe Islam should be the law in any government. She had heard a cleric say that God punished Mansour because he didn't go to the mosque and pray. Until that time, she had had no contact with any officials in Libya, but she had daily attention from the press. She told NBC she was convinced Gadhafi was responsible. After making the statement, she knew she'd overstepped her bounds. All she really knew was that Mansour had been kidnapped. Everything else was pure speculation.

Right after the interview, Gadhafi made a statement saying that Mansour was his friend and that his family was welcome in Libya. Then she received a letter from Gadhafi through the Libyan embassy in Paris, inviting her to see him. She had never been to Libya and was frightened. Thinking of her children, she knew they couldn't withstand the loss of another parent. She discussed the matter with her family and ultimately decided that she had to take the risk and go. Always savvy, she tipped off the press before she left. Her sister and her American friend Tamara, also an old friend of Mansours, accompanied her.

She told me that they flew to Jerba, Libya, and were greeted by the foreign minister. His delegation wanted to have the women ride in different cars, but they had made a pact never to separate. The three of them insisted on cramming into one vehicle. Accompanied by several cars, they were driven through the desert until they got to Tripoli, the capital, where they were put up in a luxurious hotel. Twenty-one guards stood in their hallway. Baha wasn't sure if they were protecting her from danger or if Gadhafi just didn't want her speaking with anyone. On their second day in Libya, they met dignitaries and ministers. Everyone pledged to help find Mansour, but no one had any information. Her sister-in-law (the wife of Mansour's brother) came to see her but wouldn't say anything about the kidnapping. She wanted Baha to go sightseeing, as though nothing were wrong. They went to the Mediterranean, where Mansour had always wanted to go with her.

She knew his family did not approve of her appearances in the media and her public search for Mansour. His brothers had told her it was improper for a woman to do such things, yet they did nothing themselves. The three women stayed in their room most of the time, waiting for word as to when they would see Gadhafi.

Finally, after three days, Baha asked Gadhafi's envoy to let him know that she had two children at home and that she couldn't leave them alone any longer. She respected his busy schedule, but if he couldn't see her the next day, she was leaving. At 9:30 that evening, she received a phone call that Gadhafi was ready to meet. The women rushed to dress, unsure of where the meeting would be held. Again they insisted on riding in the same car.

"We drove through Tripoli—then the street lights on the road ended. I wasn't afraid at the time, but later I wondered how I did it. I think it was because I was ready to talk. The car drove on, away from the city, and we were in the desert. No lights, nothing, for at least two hours."

At last, they came to a gate in the sand. The headlights flicked off and flashlights snapped on, held by the guards who had been waiting for them. They were taken to chairs in the sand and they sat outside. They were given something to drink in the dark. Custom dictated they drink it, whatever it was. They couldn't take the risk of insulting their host and turning it down. In the distance, Baha could see a beautiful Arabian tent with lights in it. The front was open, and it was decorated beautifully. To the left was another tent, much simpler. Then she heard a recording of the Lebanese singer Fayrouz singing a song about Damascus. Gadhafi knew she was from Damascus.

A man approached, identifying himself as a government minister, and asked Baha what she thought of their desert. She told him it was beautiful, that it reminded her of Syria. "Your moon is more beautiful than our moon," she told him. In the distance, she saw the silhouettes of what seemed to be a man and a woman. They drew closer. "Please come, please come quickly," they demanded. They walked a bit in the desert. It was dark, and they had beams from the flashlights at their feet. She looked up and saw another vague shadow in the distance. Then suddenly, Gadhafi appeared. He welcomed them and led them into the simple tent, not the beautiful one. They cautiously took their seats, encircling him.

Baha began to address Gadhafi as "Mr. President."

An aide cut her off: "Do not call him Mr. President! He is the leader of the revolution. You must call him *Qa'ed Thawra!*"

Baha turned to Gadhafi and said, "Excuse me, please, this word that he has just mentioned that I should call you—it is a scary word and I don't want to use it. It's a simple tent, there is a beautiful moon. I don't want to call you the leader of a revolution, it sounds so violent."

"You can call me what you want," he replied.

"Thank you, Mr. President," she said.

Then Gadhafi said to her, "I heard a lot about you and your interviews with the press. I know everything."

"Me, too," she replied. They laughed.

He asked her about the names and ages of her children with Mansour. When she told him that her daughter's name was Jihan, he asked if she was named after Jihan Sadat, the former First Lady of Egypt. She said no, that she was named after her mother and that Mansour loved the name. She could no longer hold back her tears.

"You know, I love Mansour very much," Gadhafi said.

"Me, too," Baha answered again. They laughed despite her tears.

"You know what I think? I think it was the CIA that took him. Mansour wasn't the opposition. He was my friend."

"No, let's speak honestly. We know he was a leader in the opposition, but there is nothing wrong with that. Opposition means, they disagree with your thoughts. It means being against certain ideas, not against you, there is nothing wrong with that. He always said you were his friend, but he disagrees with you. Remember, Mansour didn't like to fight with anyone."

Gadhafi tried to blame Mansour's disappearance on the Americans, the Egyptians, and other opposition groups. He said the Saudis would do anything for America's money. He began to ramble, saying he loved Bill Clinton because he had refused to go to Vietnam. He said he loved the American spirit at that time in history because the Americans were young and strong.

Baha broke his train of thought: "Excuse me, am I allowed to interrupt you?"

"Yes, yes," he said. She took out one of her father's books and offered him one. He thanked her, and Baha continued. "I was the same age as my son when *my* father was taken. I understand my son, my child, the way he is feeling. I am told that the bedouins have a custom: if somebody, even their enemy, holds his beard and says 'save me,' then that person must honor his request. He can't kill him. He has to save his life and protect him forever. Is that correct?"

Gadhafi said yes.

"Mr. President, are you a bedouin?"

Gadhafi nodded yes.

"Well," she said, "imagine that my son is holding your beard, that he is asking you to help find his father, inside or outside of Libya. It is your duty as a bedouin, as the president, to help him."

Gadhafi was silent.

"You know, Mr. President, I think the world is sad. It makes me feel sick and tired, so I dream. I dream of human rights and freedom of speech and a better life for all of us. Do you have dreams, Mr. President?"

"Yes, of course, I dream," he replied.

"No. I don't mean dreams when you are fast asleep. I mean daydreams, dreams where you wish the best for the world, the best for your people."

"Of course, I do."

Debbie and her mother in Fahimi Kirban's garden.

Marwan's brother Ghassan (center), 1970. Ghassan was assassinated in Beirut in 1972.

Debbie and her father
on her wedding day,
September 1982.

Marwan Kanafani and Arafat at the palace in Morocco, 1993.

Suha Arafat with Marwan (right) and journalist, Tunis, 1993.

Debbie's children at Arafat's suite in Washington, D.C., during the peace signing, 1993.

Debbie with Arafat and her daughter, Deena, at the peace signing, 1993.

Arafat, the pope, and
Marwan Kanafani in
Rome, 1992.

Marwan with President Jimmy Carter and Arafat, 1993.

Debbie, Deena, and
Tarik, Washington,
D.C., Thanksgiving
1994.

Debbie with her cousin Donna Shalala at the Tunisian Embassy in Washington, D.C., 1995.

Debbie with Baha Kikhia in Washington, D.C., 1997.

Marwan Kanafani (left) and Mansour Kikhia (center) at the United Nations, 1980.

Suha Arafat showing her child a book with Yasir Arafat's picture on the cover. Debbie Kanafani took this photo in Paris in 1997.

Debbie with Raymonda Tawil (mother of Mrs. Arafat) at Raymonda's home in Ramallah, 1998.

The engagement, Princess Dina and King Hussein, 1954.

Debbie with Queen Dina's husband, Salah Tamari (seated, center), in 1998 at the castle he built for his wife above Bethlehem. The woman between us is his cousin, and the two other men are guards.

Queen Dina at her apartment in Jordan, 1998.

Debbie Kanafani and Dr. Fahti Arafat (brother of Yasir) in the old city of Jerusalem in 1998.

Toujan al-Faisal at her apartment in Jordan,1999.

Debbie, Deena, and Tarik in Maryland in 2003.

"Do you do more than just dream of these things? Do you work for them?"

"Yes, all the time," Gadhafi said.

"Okay, when you dream, how do you see my husband? Is he dead or alive?"

Gadhafi was startled. He snapped back: "You were talking about dreams, and now you are asking me a direct question!"

He never did answer, but she wanted him to understand that she wasn't afraid to fight for her husband and that she was not going to stop looking for Mansour.

He tried to give her the impression that she could count on him. As she was leaving he asked, "Do you need anything?"

"Yes," she said. "My husband to come back."

"Everyone has their own motives," she told me as she opened the drawer of a small side table and took out a plain piece of folded white paper. She handed it me, asking me to unfold it and read it. It had no letterhead, no signature. Halfway down the page were three simple sentences. It was from the CIA. It read:

SECRET/RELEASABLE TO THE US CITIZEN FAMILY MEMBERS OF
MANSOUR KIKHIYA. WE HAVE RECEIVED CREDIBLE INFORMATION
INDICATING THAT MANSOUR WAS EXECUTED IN EARLY 1994 IN LIBYA.
IT IS OUR UNDERSTANDING FROM THIS INFORMATION THAT
MANSOUR'S REMAINS WERE DESTROYED.

Not long before our visit, two CIA agents had come to her door. She'd met with them in the past, so she invited them in. They told her they had bad news and handed her the paper. She read it and started to cry. After a moment, she regained control and wiped her eyes. She instructed the men to sit on the couch in the living room. She waved the paper in front of them. "How do I know that what is on this paper is true? If I were in a third world country, *maybe* I would expect to see a paper like this! Here I am in the United States, with what is supposed to be the most sophisticated intelligence agency in the world, and all you can do is hand me this piece of paper and expect me to accept it? Let me ask you something, gentlemen: if one of you had a loved one who was missing, would you accept a piece of paper like this as proof of their death? Would you?" The men admitted that they wouldn't, and they left.

Baha was convinced that it was a fabricated message. The CIA, she thought, was trying to build momentum against Libya. They figured that sudden knowledge of Mansour's execution by Libya would fuel world opinion and assist at the trial.

"I am learning to separate the sadness," she told me, carefully placing the paper back in the drawer. "When I look at my children, I have to think of happiness and hope. We accept life and death; we are happy when a baby is born, and we mourn and then learn to continue on after a death. The not knowing is the most difficult part."

As painful as the kidnapping was for her, the treatment by Mansour's family of her was just as bad. The men could not accept her, as a woman, being visible and active. It shamed them. They urged her to remain passive and silent. Ultimately they stopped communicating with her altogether. Since they refused to listen to her, she decided to make a video of herself, an open letter to send to his family, to Gadhafi, the Libyan cabinet ministers, the CIA, and the Egyptian secret police. She asked if I wanted to see it and popped a copy into the VCR. There she was, sitting on a simple chair in the middle of her living room, wearing a zebra print jacket, speaking directly to the camera. She said:

This is a letter to you, my husband's family and to others who try not to hear me. I want the women to listen also. Don't exclude them as you usually do, don't neglect them. My husband always told me that I had a huge family that would stand by me if something happened. Now I sit alone, hoping that at the end of this letter, we will open a new page and we will be together as a family. This is my wish, not to fight with you. I want to show you who I am. Don't judge me before you know me. Talk to me, listen to me, sit with me, then judge me. I need your help emotionally. I have the important job of raising human beings alone.

You have put your guns to my chest—men against a woman—and it is not acceptable. At the same time, I forgive you, so let's turn the page. We need each other. I may seem frightening to you because I am strong, but I am normal. When I married my husband, it was to stand beside him and give him strength if he needed it. I will continue to do this for him and for my children. I want you to know that I am no longer a woman. I have become a sword.

Baha told me to remember this on my trip to the Middle East. She said that the way to change men's treatment of women was through our sons. "Be aware," she said, "if there are differences in the way you or Marwan treat your son and your daughter. Respect starts at home. It starts with the way they see the mother."

When I left, Baha gave me a self-portrait she had painted on a large piece of silk. It had dense vibrant colors and the power of an African tribal mask—it looked as if it had the ability to scare away unwanted visitors. I planned to hang it at the entrance of my new house. No one could pass without a warning from Baha. I had no idea how much I would need this protection as I embarked on my journey.

CHAPTER EIGHT

Arriving in the Middle East

I HANDED MY PASSPORT TO THE INSPECTION OFFICER AT the Tel Aviv airport in August 1997. He stared at my name and quickly asked if I was related to Marwan Kanafani. "Yes," I said. He continued to stare, clearly expecting more of an explanation. I told him that I was visiting my children, and that seemed to be good enough. He stamped my passport and gave me a three-month visa, but not before a thorough inspection. Guards looked through my bags and were puzzled by the silverware I'd brought along, putting it through all kinds of detection machines. My explanation—that I was just bringing it with me in case I had dinner parties—made them look at me as if I was crazy. This is what probably caused them to completely disassemble my computer—and leave it that way.

I scanned the airport crowd looking for one of Marwan's drivers who had been sent to pick me up. I don't think Marwan actually absorbed that I was planning on staying for good, and I had to wonder if he'd be so eager to dispatch his driver if he knew. To him, this was just a visit. At last, I saw a man smiling and waving in my direction. He took my bags and informed me that it would take an hour or so to drive through Israel before we reached the Israeli-Palestinian border, crossing over to the West Bank, where Tarik and Deena were staying. At this border, we would go through an Israeli checkpoint, where my identity papers would be examined before being cleared for entry. On the other side of the border were various Arab towns, including my destination: Ramallah. These towns had been under Israeli occupation since the 1967 Arab-Israeli War, and now they were being handed over to Arabs for self-rule as a result of the Declaration of Principles. Israel still controlled the areas of the West Bank where there were Israeli settlements, and monitored who came in and out.

Alone in the back seat of the Land Rover, I gazed at the vast expanses of Israel's uninhabited land. There were mountains, endless and green and fertile. I couldn't help but feel perplexed by the war, why people were fighting over land when there was so much available. As we approached the Arab border towns, the lush landscape gave way to abandoned automobiles, dusty dirt roads, barefoot children, and garbage-strewn streets.

The Land Rover idled at the checkpoint. There were several small guard stations lined up like toll booths. Young Israeli soldiers, male and female, paced by, strapped with machine guns. When we were waved through without incident, I commented on how easy the passage was. There are two ways to pass through quickly, the driver told me. One was with a car that had Israeli license plates, meaning that Israelis could travel in and out of the

West Bank freely. Otherwise, the car needed government tags. Marwan's car was in the second category.

The grim scene intensified as we drove down the unpaved roads inside the West Bank. I was horrified by cows' heads hanging in front of butcher shops. People wearing tattered clothing, children clinging to them, lined up on the side of the road, waiting for transportation in the hot, sticky air. I was reminded of the refugee camps that I had seen twenty years earlier in Jordan. These people were living in the same conditions, and I thought about how shocking this must have been for my children over the summer.

As we approached Ramallah, the scenery began to match my original vision. New buildings were under construction, roads were being paved, and a few imported palm trees were fighting to survive. There were no other trees; the driver told me they had all been cut down by the Israelis during the years of conflict so that Palestinians could not hide behind them. It was also punishment, the driver believed, because a large number of people had derived their income from the olive trees, using them for olive oil. We drove up to Marwan's home, which was situated next to a newly built four-star hotel. The Grand Park Hotel had a large sign written in English and Arabic, with "Welcome" printed below it. I could see a nicely furnished restaurant patio with men and women conversing over food and drinks. This, the driver told me, was a hub for journalists and expatriates who had returned to build Palestine. Marwan's building was a recently completed, luxurious five-story apartment house that sat high on the hill, with huge balconies that overlooked the nascent city. His new wife didn't live here but remained in Tunis, where her children were being educated.

My children were thrilled to see me. We clung to one another for a few minutes while Marwan, another driver, and a guard stood silently, with cold expressions. Eventually Marwan calmed the kids and asked them to go inside. I looked around his tastefully appointed apartment, and we exchanged formal hellos. I began to tell him that I had rented a home for the children and me from a Palestinian American friend I'd known in Washington. In a detached, authoritative voice, he informed me that the children were not going anywhere, that they would live with him. I said nothing, not sure I had heard him correctly.

He told me I could not take the children from the house unless he gave me his permission and the driver accompanied me. I no longer had any right to them. I wasn't going to get any financial support. He thought I should visit them and go back to the States. Perhaps naively, I thought he would be agreeable to the idea of the children and me having our own place. I assumed it would be the way it had always been: me and the children. He had so much power at his disposal—money, status, people—all of which could be wielded against me. I had nothing. I stood speechless. He knew I had been stripped of everything, and he wanted to take my children as well.

We just stood there silently. I felt humiliated, treated like a stranger, with no recognition of the relationship I had with my children. The fact that I had practically raised them myself until that time had no bearing. I finally said that I would have them with me as had always been the case, that it would take little to support us, and they could see him every day. Marwan, his driver, and the guard continued to stare at me, three sets of eyes without compassion. I was in his land, and I had no power. There was no discussion. I knew it would be hard for me to compete with what he was giving my children financially. I could see by his home that he was lavishing them with material things. He wanted me to leave, and I knew he would not make my life easier there. I said goodbye to my children without letting on that there was any conflict. I told them I was going to find a taxi that would bring me to the new house, in a town called Bethany, so I could unpack my suitcases. They advised me to look for a taxi with yellow Israeli plates, as those cars could pass through the checkpoints without inspection. It was sweet to see them so protective. They also gave me the number of their playmate's mother. She was an American, and I think my children sensed that I might need a friend.

I stood on a dirt road, bags by my side, and waited a short time for a taxi to drive by. The streets had no names in the West Bank, so I had been told by the owner of my rented house to describe its location as "down the street from where Lazarus rose from the dead." After an hour-long trip that entailed sitting at two checkpoints, the driver proudly pointed out our holy landmark and proceeded down a dusty road. There were several nondescript cement houses, still no trees or vegetation in sight, just an overcast summer sky. We found the house after knocking on several doors. My friend's family lived in the surrounding houses, and it seemed as if they'd all been waiting to catch a glimpse of their new Western neighbor. Several of them came out to help me with my suitcases.

The house was stark: tile floors, cement walls, a large sitting room and kitchen, two bedrooms and bathrooms with updated modern facilities, as well as a large balcony that overlooked more barren hills. There was a temporary guest in the house, a student who was the son of a U.S. congressman. Fortunately he had arranged for a telephone, which was a tremendous asset because the waiting list for a phone was several months long. I looked forward to a good rest so I could wake up energetic enough to do battle with Marwan.

I planned to contact the American embassy. Surely they would enforce any U.S. agreement regarding my custody and child support. The following morning, I called the mother of Deena and Tarik's friends. I knew she was divorced from a Palestinian, who was actually a friend of Marwan. She was working in the West Bank, and I figured as an American she might be able to give me some tips. Instead, she told me that she and her husband had four children and that when they divorced, he took them. She had no rights as an American. In the beginning, he didn't even allow her to see them, so she would sneak across his garden at night to look at them through a window while they slept. Would that be me, sneaking like a thief in the night to catch a glimpse of my children? After several years, her ex-husband let the children live with her because it was simply more convenient for him.

"We are subject to the laws that govern the West Bank," she explained to me. Although civil laws were being passed as part of the new government, the laws that governed family matters and women were under the sharia, the personal status laws of the Islamic religious court. In that court, men had the right to their children after divorce once the girls were nine years old and the boys were seven years old. She warned me not to anger Marwan too much because he could take my children into the Gaza Strip, making it difficult for me to see them at all. Gaza had a stricter Islamic population and would shield my children from me, a non-Muslim. This seemed inconceivable to me.

I listened to her warnings, but in the back of my mind I assumed my situation was different because, unlike her husband, Marwan was an American citizen. I phoned the American embassy in Tel Aviv. The sympathetic woman who took my call sounded as though she had heard this story many times before. "Unfortunately," she told me, "there are no reciprocal agreements between the West Bank and the United States." She explained that in many countries, agreements upheld by American courts, including divorce and custody rulings, were enforced, but the

Palestinian government had no such rule. While in their land, Americans were subject to their laws.

This couldn't be happening. Would Marwan actually be able to take the children from me? I called Washington, D.C., and left a long message at the State Department explaining my situation. I left a U.S. voice mail number and said I would check my messages. They returned my call promptly. They were only able to confirm that what I had been told was true. The good news, according to them, was that they did have a reciprocal agreement with Israel. If I could get my children into Jerusalem, then they would work with me on a plan to escort us to the airport and put us on a plane.

I immediately rejected that idea. I wouldn't put my children through such a traumatic experience. Besides, I'd always worry that Marwan would take them back. I did not want my children to be torn by the same experiences I had had in my own childhood. I had vowed never to expose them to conflicts between Marwan and myself. I decided I would learn more about the sharia laws and perhaps find a basis on which I could win. I would also speak to people whom I had known from my marriage, the people who were now in power.

I began to make daily visits to my children at Marwan's, which was difficult due to my lack of transportation. I couldn't afford taxis, since they cost almost $100 for a round trip. For me to get to his house, I had to leave the West Bank, enter Israel for a few miles, and then reenter the West Bank. Without Marwan's help and the use of his driver or car with its special license plates, I had to take three separate public vans that were licensed to cross these borders. The vans were dirty, hot, and overcrowded. We had to wait in long lines while everyone's identity papers were inspected at the Israeli checkpoints. My trip took about two hours each way.

Although these trips were physically uncomfortable and time-consuming, I used them to observe the daily life of the Palestinians with whom I traveled. I tried to envision what it was like to be treated like them, to be deemed inferior, to have my identity papers validated every couple of hundred yards, waiting patiently for changes to take effect. Most disturbing was the humiliation of elderly passengers in front of their families at the checkpoints. They were often treated without respect, yelled at, and refused transportation for no apparent reason. I understood American poverty, but this was not only economic imbalance; this was occupation.

I wondered if Marwan thought I wouldn't be able to tolerate these trips and that I would give up and leave. But I would not leave my children, no matter how difficult the situation became. School began shortly after I arrived. The children had to go to a private school because of the language barrier. Marwan had enrolled them in a Muslim school not for religious reasons, but because it was convenient for him. The school administrators did all the paperwork for him, and the school was inside the West Bank, which meant any of the people working for him could drive them or pick them up from school; they needed no special permits. I went to the school and saw young girls covered from head to toe in black, even wearing black gloves. The education was based around religion, but I wanted my children to think critically, to question, to draw their own conclusions.

I searched for another school on my own and found the American School in Jerusalem. Attending the school would be less convenient because they would have to cross the border each day. Although Marwan and I had little communication, I convinced him that it would be better for Tarik and Deena to be in a more familiar environment. Marwan was amenable to the switch, agreeing that it would be better for the children, and one evening not long after school started, the children asked me to attend a PTA meeting. I asked Marwan if one of his drivers could take me to the school that evening. To my surprise, he agreed. I was told that a young driver and a guard would drive me; both were armed. It was dark, and I climbed into the back of a jeep to begin what I thought was going to be a short ride. I had no idea that the driver Marwan had given me was without legal papers to go into Jerusalem. Instead of the traditional route, he started driving over a rugged mountain path that Palestinians had cleared by hand for illegal passage. I was frightened in the back seat, bouncing up and down on rough terrain; my imagination started to run away with me and I began to wonder if these men had been asked to get rid of me. We made our way down a long path, which ended in a huge pile of dirt. The road had never been finished. We had to back out, with no lights to guide us, and find another path to take us over the mountain and into Jerusalem. This hair-raising journey lasted almost two hours, finally delivering me to the meeting shortly before it ended. I am sure I was pale and shaking as I introduced myself, thinking that these other parents had no idea what I had gone through just to get there. I was starting to understand that nothing would be easy in the Middle East.

When Marwan was present, he humiliated me in front of my children and demonstrated to them that I was unimportant. He showed them that he made decisions and that I would not be consulted, even with respect to such trifles as what they should eat for dinner. While my children and I were present, he would ask the maid and driver what *they* thought the children should have for dinner. They would decide, as though I were not in the room. He would then hand money to his driver, as though I couldn't be trusted to handle money at the grocery store. In front of everyone, the driver would ask Marwan if I was allowed to go in the car with the children. After a few minutes of thought, he would grant his permission. These scenarios were a challenge to me, and I learned not to show anger or respond as he wished.

One driver especially enjoyed watching Marwan treat me this way. He was a cruel man who hated my perseverance. He clearly thought that women should be home, veiled. One day, he had driven my children and me into town. My daughter and I got out of the car after the driver pulled over. We stood on the street looking in a store window when the driver began shouting at me from across the street. *"Yalla, yalla!"* he yelled, indicating he wanted us to hurry up. There was no reason to rush; he simply wanted to be rude and controlling. I got into the back of the car with my daughter and told him not to yell at me like that again. He began cursing at me, so I grabbed my daughter and got out of the car with her. We took a taxi back to Marwan's house with him following us in his car. The driver was furious.

A few days later, a close friend of Marwan came to see me at Marwan's house, where I was still visiting almost every day, under the close eye of his staff. He told me that the driver had come to him and told him that I was having men meet me at Marwan's house. I told him that was untrue and I called in the maids, who were always present, to confirm it. The man explained that he believed me and thought the angered driver was trying to start rumors for revenge.

The way this driver was raised, the worst thing anyone could do to a woman was to start rumors about her with men. In his village, young unmarried girls were punished by honor killings for this kind of behavior. In an "honor killing," a father, brother, or other male family kills a female relative accused of dishonoring the family through improper relations with a man. She was killed, the rationale went, to save her family's honor. Marwan's friend was kind enough to speak with Marwan about the situation. Marwan never discussed it with me, but he did assign a different driver to my children. This was one of his few acts of support. He didn't want me there, but at the same time I think it was a relief that I was nearby to look after the children at his convenience, because he was always busy with work. Those days always ended awkwardly for me. I would collect my things like an outsider and say goodbye to my children.

When the children were in school, I set up meetings with people whom I thought could offer me custody advice. I contacted the local United Nations offices addressing women's issues. They set up a meeting for me, where I learned more about the laws of sharia. There are five major schools of thought on sharia. Some schools take a more literal approach to the Koran, the Islamic holy book, and some have a looser interpretation. The amount of sharia incorporated into civil law varies from country to country. The sharia come from a combination of sources, including the Koran, the Hadith (the sayings and conduct of Prophet Mohammed in the holy Koran), the *fatwas* (the rulings of Islamic scholars), and *giyas*, which use analogies to solve problems not already addressed. Therefore, there is plenty of room for interpretation.

Many countries adhere to an interpretation that in marriage, the husband pledges his support of the woman in return for obedience. Men can use physical force against disobedient wives. In most countries, women cannot work if the husband forbids it. The husband has the unilateral right to divorce his wife without cause. I realized that this was the reason women I met would often say, "You seem nice. Why would Marwan divorce you?" They assumed Marwan initiated the divorce, because in their culture they knew no other way.

There are limited circumstances that allow a woman to divorce a man, for instance, if he has a contagious skin disease like leprosy. In some reform countries like Egypt and Iran, a woman can divorce and sue for failure to provide financial support. However, I was told that it can take years to get a court date, and when that date arrives, men are typically ordered to pay only several dollars a month. In divorce, children traditionally belong to their father, but their mother can care for them when they are very young, usually under the age of seven. The age the mother loses the rights to her children varies from country to country. Women can inherit property, but men automatically inherit twice as much.

I wondered why a system would separate a mother from her child and leave her with no means of support. In my case, it was worse, because I am not Muslim, and my children were considered Islamic property despite Marwan's lack of religious observance.

I needed some help navigating my way through this new culture. First, I needed to figure out a way to support myself. I had to be practical because to respond emotionally would be the beginning of defeat. I did my best to stay disengaged from power struggles with Marwan. I stayed focused on my purpose, which was to be with my children. I decided to call Suha Arafat and her mother, Raymonda, who were back in the Gaza Strip, about two hours from Ramallah. Arafat's headquarters were in Gaza, and many of the government offices were there.

Raymonda and Suha insisted I visit them as soon as possible so we could figure out a strategy to handle this situation. Suha and her mother still disliked Marwan and fought him on many fronts. I told my children I was going to the Gaza Strip to visit Raymonda for a few days. I learned Marwan had an apartment in the same building. In fact, they would be leaving to go there at the same time as me. But Marwan refused to allow me to ride with them.

It took me close to a full day to make the trip from Ramallah to Gaza using public transportation. I left in the morning, taking a small, crowded taxi for several hours to the Eritz checkpoint at the entrance to the Gaza Strip. Egypt had lost control of the Gaza Strip to Israel during the Six Day War of 1967. During the 1970s and 1980s, the Israeli government had appropriated land to build Israeli settlements and strengthen their presence there. Resentment stemming from occupation and a weak economy and a large refugee population made the region a center for Palestinian activism and political unrest.

The 1994 peace agreement had called for limited self-rule in the Gaza Strip, allowing the Palestinians to manage Palestinian affairs while Israel maintained control over Israeli settlements. It was difficult for Palestinians to get permission from the Israeli government to leave Gaza, except for day work permits. The entrance to Gaza resembled a prison, with barbed-wire fences, towers with artillery pointed in all directions, machine guns hanging over young soldiers' arms. Cars were allowed only to a certain point, unless they had VIP plates, usually reserved for high-ranking government officials. Then Palestinians had to take your luggage and walk through what was called no-man's-land, a stretch of land running about a quarter of a mile. At the end bordering Israel was an Israeli checkpoint. Halfway along the walk to the end of no-man's-land was a second Israeli checkpoint and a facility to sweep cars for bombs at the discretion of the Israeli soldiers. I waited in long lines with Palestinians to explain to Israelis why I wanted to enter the Gaza Strip. As I came closer to taking my turn, the Israeli guard, thinking I was a Palestinian, started yelling at me to give her my papers. I took out my passport, slammed it on the table, and told her not to talk to me that way. She was shocked to learn I was an American. She immediately made a phone call, and several minutes later, another Israeli soldier came dashing over and apologetically led me to another location, where people holding American passports trickled through. I was sure that while I had been waiting with Palestinians on the unpleasant line, Marwan had zipped through the area in his motorcade with ease.

At the other end of no-man's-land was a checkpoint run by Palestinians. They, as part of the peace process, got to control the last 100 feet of no-man's-land. It was more of a symbolic gesture than anything else, since one had to pass through so much Israeli security before getting there. Israelis who lived in the settlements took a different route. When I made it into Palestinian territory, I saw Palestinian soldiers in their new uniforms, a consequence of the peace signing. I also saw no fewer than ten taxis pleading for my business. I had no address, but I figured it would be enough to tell a taxi driver that I was going to the home of Raymonda Tawil. I tried to communicate the best I could in Arabic with the driver. He indicated he knew where to go.

The Gaza Strip, also under construction, was a combination of refugee camps and villas, veiled women on donkeys and shiny new Mercedes, all bordering the beautiful blue Mediterranean. I knew that the building Raymonda and Marwan lived in was across from the sea. I also knew it was next to Arafat's home and under his security. Several of Arafat's ministers had residences in this building as well. The driver became frustrated as he was trying to find his way around security to get closer. Through the window, I saw a man who seemed unusually sure of himself strutting down the street. I instructed the driver to pull up so that I could ask him if he knew how we could get closer to Raymonda's home. I rolled down the window and asked. He looked at me suspiciously and asked who I was, why I wanted to know. I told him that I was Marwan Kanafani's wife (I did *not* say "former") and that I was looking for Raymonda Tawil.

"You are Marwan Kanafani's wife?" he asked incredulously.

"Yes," I said.

"I am Marwan Kanafani's bodyguard!" I wasn't sure if I

should be happy or upset. Somehow I had managed to single out one of Marwan's bodyguards in a population of 800,000. Not sure whether he should believe me, he began to test me.

"How many children do you have?"

"Two, a boy and a girl."

"What sport does your son like?"

"Basketball."

"Okay, you are the mother. I take your son to play basketball sometimes. I will show you where the house is." He took my things from the taxi and drove me to Raymonda's. He took me past her security into the elevator and right into the living room of her apartment. This man, one of the many enlightened men I met while on my journey, became a true friend and helped me during difficult times.

I was overwhelmed with relief the moment I saw Raymonda. I wanted to climb out of the shell I'd built for myself and let her take over. She was better at this than I was. She paced back and forth in her large, comfortable apartment on the eighth floor overlooking the Mediterranean. It had marble floors, a large salon, and sliding pocket doors leading out to several seaside balconies. We could have been at a resort if it weren't for the army tanks downstairs and the armed guards in the lobby, on the elevator, and outside the apartment door. Once again, I was confused by all of the protection. The guards weren't protecting us from Israelis. It was a relatively peaceful time. It was Hamas fundamentalists who were now the enemy, those who didn't agree with the Palestinian government representatives who lived in this building.

I could tell by her fury that I had become her next cause as I began to tell her about my predicament. Remembering her own separation from her mother, she vowed to declare war against Marwan and make sure that I would be able to stay in the country for as long as my children were there. We would go to Arafat's home the next day, so I could discuss the situation with Suha.

In the meantime, Raymonda was calling in her local allies, starting with Abu Hussein, a minister in Arafat's government who lived across the hall. A thin man with a huge mustache and a stylish pinstriped suit, he was married to a biologist who was a professor at the local university. His family was in hiding, threatened by Hamas fundamentalists who were offended because he'd allowed men and women to sit together during concerts held at a hotel that he owned. Abu Hussein was trying to create events that could bring joy and relief to people, but others thought it could encourage improper relationships between men and women.

I knew my children were in the building, upstairs at Marwan's apartment, and I had asked them to visit me at Raymonda's. Shortly after I arrived, my son came to the door, escorted by a guard. He sat next to me on her couch, his head on my shoulder, his arms wrapped around me. Raymonda kept asking the minister to help me, telling him to look at my son and how he loves his mother. I could sense that he was sympathetic but that Raymonda was asking him to solve a problem out of his reach. Shortly after, Marwan's guard returned to take my son back. It broke my heart to know that my children were on another floor in the same building and I couldn't be with them.

Raymonda's phone rang in Gaza as much as it had in Paris. She listened to complaints about the government, the lack of travel permits, money, failing businesses, imprisoned relatives. Some called because she was the mother-in-law of the president and had a sympathetic ear; others were long-time friends hoping she would speak out. She was often teary-eyed when she spoke about local conditions and the people she had to stand up against, but she refused to be defeated. She was a one-woman mobile revolution, always finding a little more strength to keep her going.

We sat down for dinner with Abu Hussein, and a maid placed a bowl of food on the table, cheerfully announcing that a woman had brought the food to the guards downstairs as a gift for Raymonda. As I was thinking that this was a nice gesture of appreciation, Raymonda quickly jumped up and removed the dish from the table, telling me it could be poisoned food. I had not yet developed the paranoia that was so natural in this part of the world. I noticed that the security and precautions to protect government people from fundamentalists was much stronger in the Gaza Strip than in Ramallah and other parts of the West Bank. Gaza had been less integrated with the outside world than the rest of the West Bank. Life in the Gaza Strip was marked by harsher conditions, more poverty and refugee camps, less freedom of movement. Many people had never been allowed to leave this small peninsula and had lived their entire lives under occupation.

The frustration and lack of hope that washed over their lives created a fertile climate for a reliance on God, not people, to save them. Fundamentalist leaders were the only allies they had, supplying the few social services, medical assistance, and educational opportunities that existed. Westerners and Western thought represented occupation. In their minds, the weapons that were used against them, the policies that ignored their rights, all originated from and were supported by Western thought. Now Arafat had returned, and he had to show his people that life under the Declaration of Principles would be different for them. If he couldn't prove it, Hamas, the fundamentalists, would just grow stronger.

After dinner, I asked a guard if he would follow me while I took a walk outside. This was against Raymonda's advice, and I understood why from the commotion of cars honking at me, driven by fundamentalists who were offended by my lack of covering. I came back and stayed confined to two large balconies, where I could observe without fear. I could see fishermen in little wooden boats, soldiers in uniforms on a large rooftop practicing their march, and Arafat's helicopter landing pad in full view. He lived like a bird, airborne all the time.

The following day was Mother's Day in Palestine. My plan was to go to Suha Arafat's for lunch. But that night I sank into a deep sleep and was jolted awake in the early morning by the sound of loud knocking on the front door. I came out of my bedroom at the same time as Raymonda, and we rushed to her front door. The guard outside the door yelled that it was okay to open it. In walked four handsome young men in uniform with M16 machine guns slung over their shoulders, carrying a large basket of flowers. "Happy Mother's Day!" they declared to Raymonda. A gift from President and Mrs. Arafat. Raymonda was thrilled with her Mother's Day present, not thinking twice how unusual this little scene was.

I walked up the street accompanied by two guards to visit Suha. We were within Arafat's government compound, so the streets weren't clogged with outside traffic. There was an abundance of barricades, tanks, and Palestinian soldiers. We approached the simple, small, square-shaped white building that Arafat and his wife called home. I caught a glimpse of a swing set on a patch of grass on the other side of a military tank. I entered a small, poorly lit foyer with a narrow wooden staircase in front of me and a door to the side. The door led to Arafat's quarters and the stairs led to Suha's newly built apartment. Arafat was not at home, so I asked the guards if I could see his quarters before going upstairs, and they agreed. They would never insult me by asking to look in my purse or question the reason for my visit. The guards inside his living quarters let me roam around because they knew I was the mother of Marwan's children. It was dark; there were few windows for security reasons. There was a small sitting area for several soldiers and two small sparsely furnished bedrooms. One was Arafat's, and one was for guards to rest in shifts. There was no difference in the size or decor in Arafat's or the guard's rooms. All of the rooms were minimally decorated with worn-out furnishings.

Suha's part of the house, upstairs, was bright, with many windows and a terrace. Those able to peek over the six-foot wall surrounding the terrace could glimpse the Mediterranean. The interior was one large room that served as a living and dining area. Suha had two cozy sitting areas in the living room, furnished with comfortable sofas and off to the side a dining table that seated ten people. There were two small bedrooms—one for her daughter, Zahwa, and her nanny, and one for her.

Suha wanted to know how my children were and all about my situation with Marwan. When I told her that Marwan would not allow the children to live with me, she was furious. She immediately suggested that I have breakfast the next morning with Arafat, who was known to get involved in family matters like this. I was reluctant, because I knew that Marwan would never be persuaded by Arafat, and he would only get angry. I told her what would be helpful would be to speak with Arafat about allowing me to have a position at the local television station. I needed to support myself, and I knew the work would be interesting. To my relief, she told me that this could be arranged.

Then Suha told me that someone at odds with Marwan had given her a chapter of a book Marwan was secretly writing about Arafat, criticizing some of his decisions. The person wanted Suha to give the chapter to Arafat in order to punish Marwan. Suha took the chapter and saved it in her little war chest, never handing it over to her husband. Suha was willing to hand it over now if I wanted to let Marwan know she had it. Surprised, I let her know I appreciated the offer, but I couldn't resort to those tactics. I believed the bond these men had would allow them to override any sense of betrayal. This could very likely backfire, making Marwan even angrier.

A mutual friend of ours, a young woman whom I had met in the States many years earlier, was also having lunch with us. Suha seemed lively and ready to enjoy some conversation unrelated to politics. The phone rang in the living room, and Suha picked it up. It was a friend of the president, and he wanted to know where Arafat was. Suha claimed not to have any idea. She hung up and told us that even when a friend of Arafat's called, she couldn't disclose his whereabouts for security reasons. Suha resumed her enthusiastic chatter and asked the guest to share some details about her new boyfriend. "Well, he is Iraqi, but he is against Saddam Hussein," she said. I told her that I'd like to meet him sometime and asked where he was. She said she couldn't tell me because he was in hiding. The three of us started laughing about the state of romance in the Middle East.

We continued to enjoy simple girl talk, worlds away from the tanks and guards on the other side of the door, until I commented to Suha that I had seen some public pools on my drive through the Gaza.

"Yes," Suha said. "The problem is that we intended to have a secular society where people could be free and not ruled by the fundamentalists. Now they are threatening people, frightening them, especially the women who have been fighting against them. They are making them swim completely covered with long sleeves and leggings. The more the United States doesn't support us, the more these fundamentalists can strengthen their movement. They can try to turn people against our new government because we believed in America's support."

Suha Arafat was too outspoken for that little strip of land. Unsure of how to keep her quiet, the men around her husband relied on the unlikely hope that she would stay in Tunis or France and forget about the war-torn area. "I don't take directions from anyone. This is what scares the men around my husband the most. They are not accustomed to a woman like me," she said. I believed it.

My short visit was ending, and Suha asked her driver to take me to the border. This was as far as he was permitted to go. He drove so fast that I held onto the seat in front of me for dear life. There is no such thing as a leisurely ride in Palestine: everyone drives as though they are under fire.

We passed a refugee camp, and I asked him to stop and escort me inside. He seemed startled by my request, asking me to repeat it several times before he agreed. I had never seen conditions like these before. People were living in homes made out of cardboard. They were friendly, and I was trailed by barefoot children in tattered clothing who wanted their photo taken. They had just made a kite out of newspapers and discarded objects. I asked them if I could buy the kite from them. They were thrilled. Word quickly spread, and all the children from the camp came running. I gave them a few dollars and left with my kite. When I arrived back at the border, the Israeli soldiers didn't know if they should allow me to pass through with my new purchase. Eventually they let me go home. I hung the kite from my bedroom ceiling and hoped that Suha could help change the lives of the children who made it.

CHAPTER NINE

Finding My Way

SUHA ARAFAT SUGGESTED I MEET WITH THE MINISTER OF broadcasting, Radwan Abu Ayiash. My friend Bassam Abu Sharif arranged it and accompanied me for the introduction. Bassam and Marwan's relationship had soured over the years as Bassam, who used to hold Marwan's position, felt that Marwan had built a wedge between him and Arafat in order to win Arafat's favor. Bassam was an icon of the PLO and had been on a path of reconciliation, even writing a book with a prominent Israeli journalist, entitled *Best of Enemies*.

When I first arrived in Ramallah, I had gone to Bassam's home to see him and he offered his support and protection in a very brotherly way. I often visited him, and we chatted alone in his kitchen as he cooked chicken for me. Occasionally we were interrupted by one of the many armed men in army fatigues who roamed around his house. I wondered who provided his protection. I gathered it was Arafat. One day over lunch, he told me that he had felt betrayed by Marwan and was disappointed by his willingness to take Bassam's position after winning Arafat's trust. "I've faced many dangers in life," he told me, "but nothing scares me more than friends who betray you or people who forget what they have said."

He occupied himself pursuing work as a writer and as a supporter of peace by calling for a laying down of arms. He told me that once he was staying in a hotel in Rome and found out that a man who had ordered his death was also in the hotel. Bassam called him and asked if he could meet him and shake his hand for peace. Bassam demonstrated this, holding out his hand with only three fingers left. Now his enemies were the Palestinian militants who thought he had sold out. As I was leaving his house one afternoon, I had a bag with me filled with food items I had bought in the Jewish side of Jerusalem earlier that day. Bassam called to me as I picked up my bag and was about to walk out. He told me to wait a moment while he rushed back in the kitchen. He took my bag and moved the contents to another bag from his closet. I was puzzled. He smiled and said he didn't want me to get shot at while leaving, pointing to the Hebrew printed on the bag I was carrying from Jerusalem.

Now, in another protective gesture, he was coming with me to make sure the minister, an old friend of his, gave me what I needed: a job. As we sat on the patio of the Grand Park Hotel, Bassam pointed out the approaching minister, who used a cane and walked with a limp. Bassam mentioned it was due to an injury sustained during six years in an Israeli prison. "For what?" I asked. He casually said it was part of a roundup; all the men in his village had been taken to prison. Then he told me that he did not get along with Marwan either, which I thought could help me. I realized that some people disliked Marwan because of his abrasive style, some were jealous of his close relationship with Arafat, and others did not agree with his efforts on behalf of peace. I also realized that I had to be careful that the same people didn't use me to get back at him.

The minister agreed to hire me as a director of international productions. I would work with the United Nations and various countries producing TV shows to impart messages of human rights, women's and children's rights, and health education. My shows would air over Nilesat, a satellite service reaching twenty-two Arab countries and part of North Africa. All this, and the highest salary given to a government worker besides a member of parliament: $1,200 per month. There was one catch: Arafat would have to personally sign papers to approve my position.

Raymonda had taken up residence at her apartment in Ramallah, the same place she'd stayed while under house arrest twenty years earlier. With customary Arab hospitality, she invited me to stay with her for as long as I liked, which made it much easier to see my children, since her home was close to Marwan's. During the time that I stayed with her, there were always a minimum of seven or eight visitors present, all anxious to discuss current affairs. Raymonda relayed my custody situation to each person who came through the door.

Her living room was filled with photos. One in particular caught my eye. Raymonda was posing with a woman who looked just like folk singer Joan Baez, an icon of my youth. I asked her who the woman was, thinking perhaps I was mistaken. "That's a woman from the United States who came here and wrote a song about me," she said, laughing. Of all her famous admirers, it was Joan Baez who impressed me most.

Meanwhile, Arafat signed my papers, and I reported to work right away, without hassle. Marwan never commented on my new career. I think he was surprised, but he never openly criticized me. The TV station was down a long dirt road, crowded with children playing Roadblock, a favorite game of the time: they would set up fake checkpoints, and some of the children would pretend to be Israeli soldiers, and some would be Palestinians. The building itself looked like it had been barraged by bombs. Armed guards were either sitting outside the entrance on folding chairs or else planting rosebushes in the soil, weapons slung over their backs.

Inside, the industrial green paint peeling off the walls was pocked with bullet holes. My new office was up five flights of chipped linoleum stairs. Everyone was crammed into tiny offices, except for the minister, who had a spacious domain with a waiting room outside. On my first day, he explained that the television station had two opposing camps in it. The larger side supported Arafat and the types of programming we would do: shows that supported peace by covering the peace efforts, interviews with Israelis and Palestinians who supported peace, shows that were educational for women and supported their knowledge of health issues and laws so they could be informed and thus empowered. Our shows featured actresses wearing modern clothes, conversing with men in social settings, unlike the segregation that the conservative religious people preferred. The other camp was a much smaller group, supported by Hamas. They favored shows that undermined the peace process and supported militant action against Israel. Radwan Abu Ayiash warned me that I would have opposition, that I might encounter resistance, but he let me know I would have protection and pledged his support. With those warnings out of the way, the minister invited me to attend a party that evening to celebrate the one-year anniversary of the television station, where he planned to announce my arrival to the team.

That evening, my taxi couldn't get close to the building where the party was being held due to heavy security. Arafat was attending, along with his entourage of guards. I wove in and out of army tanks on the poorly lit streets on foot, until finally I made my way inside. Arafat was speaking on a bare stage, surrounded by men in army fatigues, berets, and sunglasses, M16s at the ready. After a quick speech in Arabic (which I couldn't understand, but judging from the audience's reaction, assumed was a pep talk of some kind), I was approached by the head of one of the TV departments. Since I would be the new director of international productions, he wanted to know if I would read a speech regarding the type of programming that would air on the Palestinian TV network. He had it written in English and said a translator would accompany me to convey it in Arabic. The speech itself would air over Palestinian TV. I appreciated his willingness to include me, and I agreed. He handed it to me, and I began to skim it before stepping up to the podium. I realized that it had a militant slant toward Hamas, calling on my "brothers and sisters in prison to rise up and protest." There was no way I could stand up and read such words. I had been set up. The man who had given me the speech had wanted me, the ex-wife of Marwan Kanafani, to read a speech supporting Hamas to humiliate Marwan. I searched for the minister to show him what had been given to me. When I found him and he read the speech, he agreed with me. Everything in this region was politicized, and I was learning to proceed with great caution.

Since I now had a job, I was able to move into my own place, closer to my children. I found an apartment across the valley that directly overlooked Marwan's building. I saw the children regularly at Marwan's home. They called it *their* home, and that was difficult for me. A month into my job, the minister arranged for me to see a prominent religious sheik. In terms of marriage and family, there was only the religious court; family law didn't fall under the rubric of civil court. I vividly remember the sheik's long white beard and his pained expression when listening to my complaints. He never once looked at me as I told him that I wanted my children back, that I needed the support of the religious court. He expressed no sympathy, just silence. Finally, he commented that I might be entitled to some financial support and that I should request to be heard in front of the court.

I called a lawyer I had been introduced to through the United Nations office. Not surprisingly, he said he had never seen a woman win in court. He warned me that they would try to destroy my character, and I would end up with nothing.

I also knew that the problem was not mine alone. I tried to see beyond my own situation and befriended local women. One friend, a worker for UNIFEM, took me to visit an orphanage run by nuns in Bethlehem. The nuns were protecting young girls who were in danger of being victims of honor killings because they had become pregnant.

Organizations such as Amnesty International and the United Nations Development Fund for Women (UNIFEM), which provides financial and technical assistance to foster women's empowerment, all agree that there are no reliable statistics on honor killings. It's difficult to collect data because people are fearful of retaliation by family members. Some estimate that there are probably 100 honor killings a year in Palestine and 200 to 400 killings per year in larger countries. A Palestinian human rights group surveyed Palestinian men in 1997, and 25.3 percent agreed that family had the right to kill a female family member who had shamed them. In the Arab world, an individual's behavior affects the perception of the entire family: if a girl does something shameful, the whole family is disgraced. The woman's identity is tied to her relationship within a family so strongly that it's even reflected in the names she is given throughout her life. She is known as "the daughter of . . . ," then as "the wife of . . . ," then as "the mother of . . .." If her behavior is shameful, the family must kill the shame.

We passed old monasteries, and along the way decided to stop at one. It was in an enormous building perched atop ruins from the Roman Empire. Franciscan monks, most of whom had taken the vow of silence, lived there. A young Lebanese man who worked in the store told me he was finishing his doctorate in theology and studying the ancient handwritten books in the library. We discovered that our families were from the same town in the mountains of Lebanon. He treated me like a long-lost friend and invited my girlfriend and me to have lunch with the monks.

We walked through the dark, silent halls to a simple room off the kitchen and took our seats at the table with ten monks, all of whom remained silent. My new friend, however, talked a lot and was extremely charming. After lunch, he called someone to show my friend around the monastery and said he wanted to show me the garden. As soon as we were alone, he told me that he was really there because he was aligned with a Lebanese Christian general. He collected information from both Palestinians and Israelis about what was going on inside Lebanon. He wanted to know if I was interested in helping his cause, since we were from the same place. He thought I would be the perfect spy. I wasn't quite sure how to decline a spying offer, but fortunately my friend reappeared a few minutes later. I said goodbye as nonchalantly as possible.

Bethlehem was such a peaceful place, with beautiful, uneven stone buildings. It seemed impossible that this ancient land was at the heart of so much strife. We parked and walked down a steep cobblestone street toward the orphanage. I stuck my head through one doorway and saw Russian monks, recognizable by their long beards, inside a room made of stone, hand-dipping candles, each one tending to a steaming cauldron. An old episode of *I Love Lucy* crackled on a black-and-white TV in the background.

At the end of the street, we reached large wooden doors with a peephole. We rang the bell, and when my friend was recognized, we were permitted entry. The building was immaculate. It was clear that this was a caring, loving place for children. There were toys and little playrooms. Children were being held and fed. I played with the children and was impressed by the love and care that they got.

The pregnant women took shelter here for good reason. In one instance, the brother of a pregnant girl had come to the convent saying that he missed his sister and wanted to comfort her. The sisters believed him and brought the pregnant young woman to the door, then left to give the siblings some privacy. As soon as they were out of sight, he shot and killed her.

I did not meet or see any pregnant women. I was told they were there, behind securely locked doors. I did not ask to see the girls they were hiding—I respected what they were doing and their privacy. I did meet one woman working at the orphanage who was trying to make honor killings punishable by law. Even today, the toughest sentence for an honor killing is six months in prison. This woman invited me to meet some of her friends in Gaza, girls who were trying to change the laws pertaining to this crime. I traveled there a few days later.

My first stop was at a small home, where I met several women, whose names I promised not to reveal. They took their head coverings off when they were inside the house, and they wore jeans. One proudly told me she was divorced, with her parents' approval. The girls told me they were forming an underground movement to fight fundamentalists, and they needed help. They wanted to know if I would be a liaison between members of their group who lived in different towns. They couldn't travel freely between towns due to political restrictions, and communication between them was difficult. Cell phones were expensive, and phone lines were hard to come by. I agreed to help them, since I could travel more freely between towns (though travel was still challenging). My job would be to inform each group what the other was doing. I would also stay in touch with several people who were willing to take pregnant girls in. Women were targets: if they were seen talking to men, they could be killed. If they became pregnant by rape, they could be killed. Rumors flew, and nowhere was safe.

Before I left, one woman read a poem written by an Algerian girl named Meena just before she was assassinated by fundamentalists in her own country:

I am the woman who has awoken
My voice had mingled with thousands of arisen women
My fists are clenched with the fists of a thousand compatriots
To break together all these sufferings, all these fetters of slavery
I'm the woman who has awoken
I've found my path and will never return

These women seemed to look up to me, perceiving me as a liberated Western woman, but it was I who was impressed and inspired by them.

I went to see a group of young girls about fourteen years old, whom my new friends had asked me to call on in Ramallah. The meeting was arranged by one of their mothers. The girls were going into villages under the pretense of speaking about health issues and talking to other teenage girls about honor killings. Once alone, they let girls know that if they were a victim of incest or felt they were about to become the victim of a vicious rumor, or if their brothers or father began to accuse them of the kind of wrongdoing that could lead to an honor killing, their group could provide protection and a secret shelter for them. These young girls were risking their lives. If they were caught, they or their families could suffer severe punishment by the Islamic court. They could be seen as apostates, a crime punishable by execution, or they could be the victims of an honor killing themselves if they shamed the family.

Um Jihad, the minister of social welfare in the new Palestinian government, was also trying to help these girls. Um Jihad was one of the PLO's icons, and I'd made a point of speaking to her at the ministry. In 1959, she had been the first woman to join Fatah, the political organization founded by Arafat and her husband, Abu Jihad, which later was the largest portion of the PLO. Her name was an alias meaning "mother of the struggle," and her husband's name, Abu Jihad, also an alias, means "father of the struggle." I was glad to see that this stalwart of the PLO hadn't forgotten these defenseless women. In 1966, when the Syrian president failed at his efforts to gain control of the Fatah Party, he threw four of the leaders in jail for one month, including Arafat and her husband. While they were imprisoned, she led the movement herself.

Um Jihad conveyed to me how, twenty years later, in the 1970s, while they were living in Tunis, a female journalist had come to their home to interview Abu Jihad. They spent the afternoon together, and then she left in the early evening. It was Ramadan, and they had let most of their security staff go home early. That night, Abu Jihad sat at his desk in their bedroom working while she rested in bed with her youngest child sleeping next to her. Alarmed by a loud noise, Abu Jihad grabbed his gun. Um Jihad joined him, and together they opened the bedroom door. Tiptoeing down the hallway, they were startled when a group of armed, masked men surrounded them. Some grabbed her, some grabbed him, and another one ran down the hall, opened her bedroom door, and fired a shot. Her older children began to run from their rooms but were ordered back by the assassins. Abu Jihad was shot eighty-three times while she watched. Afterward one of participants who had been videotaping the events (presumably for later viewing) removed her mask. It was the woman who had been posing as a journalist earlier that day. Abu Jihad had been one of the Mossad's most sought-after men in Arafat's crowd. The best way to hurt Arafat was to kill those closest to him.

Some say this was done to humiliate Um Jihad since she had naively opened her home to the woman in the first place. Some say it was to humiliate Abu Jihad with the fact that a woman had been part of his assassination. At the time, there was much tension between Israelis and Palestinians. Abu Jihad was believed to have been starting an uprising in the West Bank and Gaza Strip. He was Arafat's closest aide and headed all the PLO military operations. In 1997, Israel's *Maariv* newspaper published a report that the killing had been overseen by the deputy military chief, Ehud Barak, who became prime minister of Israel in 1999.

Arafat had appointed several of the wives of his most loyal murdered men to prominent positions. Although Um Jihad was known to wear a scarf around her neck with her husband's picture printed on it, she dressed in conservative knit suits, hair short and makeup and jewelry perfect. She had big dreams for social reform. She was involved in raising money for shelters to protect young girls who were victims of incest and rape. In Arafat's eyes, women and men were equal, but he couldn't impose his views because it would cause a more severe fundamentalist backlash.

Shortly after my trip to Bethlehem, I received a call from the American consulate saying that my cousin Donna Shalala had instructed them to find me because she was taking a trip to Israel and the West Bank. She would be meeting with Um Jihad to discuss health issues of the Palestinians and then would go to Gaza to meet with President and Mrs. Arafat.

I met Donna in Jerusalem after she completed these two visits. She told me that she discussed with Um Jihad the issue of iodine deficiencies and the high number of goiters this caused. The salt that Palestinians received was kosher and therefore didn't have iodine. Her meeting with the Arafats amused her. She said that she arrived in Gaza, first to meet with Suha; then Arafat would follow. They sat in a room together, cameras and film rolling. Having a cabinet minister from the United States visit Gaza was unprecedented. They sat down and Donna asked, "Where is my cousin's husband?" I hadn't told Mrs. Arafat that Donna was my cousin, so Suha didn't know what she meant. When Donna told her "Marwan Kanafani," Suha went into a frenzy. "What? Debbie is your cousin? I didn't know! Do you know what Marwan has done to her?" Suha spent the rest of their visit on a rampage about Marwan. When Arafat entered, Suha introduced Donna as "Debbie Kanafani's cousin," never mentioning her official position.

I periodically tried to ask Marwan if the children could stay overnight at my house, but he would not agree. One day I had rented some movies for my children at the American Consulate video service and library in Jerusalem. I called them from the television station and told them. They were very excited. I took advantage of the situation and asked if they would like to come to my apartment to pick them up. They'd never been there; Marwan wouldn't allow it. This was the first (and last) time they ever came. I figured with this ploy that they would convince Marwan to let them be driven. They called me back saying that Riyad, their driver, would take them over in the early evening. I made it clear that I wanted them to visit with me for a little while. Of course, I secretly wished that they would feel so at home they would go back to Marwan and insist on living with me, of their own accord. But when they came in, they acted formal, as if they were at a stranger's home, sitting stiffly on the sofa. I broached the subject of why our lives had changed completely. I explained what had happened to my father. They had known about the trial, but now, since they were a bit older, I could explain in more detail. I told them that after the trial, all of our money was frozen, that I no longer had a way to support us, that their grandfather was still incarcerated. I explained that this is why they'd been sent abroad and that I had come as soon as possible to join them. They listened with surprise and told me they hadn't understood the circumstances. They had just been told by their father that we thought it was best they live with him. I felt they understood my struggle to be there.

I continued learning about the area and doing what little I could. I went to see a theater group that was traveling to different schools. They were teaching teens to examine traditional family roles. They would play out a scene with a dominant male figure and a submissive female. After the scene was played out, they would allow other members of the student audience to come on stage and replace the actors, creating their own dialogue with different, more positive endings. The young people had very different attitudes and did not accept the roles of the older generation.

Following this lead, I was given the opportunity by UNICEF to make several TV spots encouraging education for girls. One spot featured two girls walking to school approaching another girl who was hanging laundry. They looked at each other in silence, then urged her to put down her laundry basket and accompany them. The girl put her basket down and then scrawled on a sheet hanging in the wind: "This is not my future." Much of this work was done on location. The office environment was a bit hostile; it was obvious that the Hamas employees disliked me. They'd often take equipment from me, not have cars available when I needed them for a shoot, or linger in the editing rooms when I was scheduled to use them. They gave me the cold shoulder in the hallways and ignored me when I spoke. Not surprisingly, this TV spot didn't do anything to help our relations. I was eventually summoned by the American consulate in Jerusalem. They wanted to know what I was doing at the television station. "You'll never get out of the West Bank alive," one of the attachés cautioned. I wasn't frightened. If the women who lived here were brave enough to speak out against the rules they wanted changed, then I could be, too.

After I spent eight months abroad, my visa was about to expire, and I faced the possibility that it would not be renewed. Visas in Palestine were under the jurisdiction of Israel, and the television station was trying to get me a work permit. The minister of broadcasting said he would take me to a Palestinian government official who had close ties with the Israelis to resolve the situation. Again, it was useful that Marwan was not on good terms with this man. I went to his office and after the customary tea, the minister explained that I needed to stay in Palestine because of my children and my work. The official told me that my visa could be renewed only if I left the country and then returned. Upon my return, they could decide if I would be issued a one-, two-, or three-month visa. The gentleman told me that he was allowed a few privileged visas, meaning that he needed only to give the Israelis a name, and they would issue an extended visa. The catch was that I would still have to leave the country and come back in. On my arrival, though, I would be issued a six-month work permit visa.

I was grateful for this favor and decided to use this as a chance to take a short trip to Italy to see my stepmother, who was visiting Montecatini, a small town in Tuscany. I told my children I was leaving for a week, but they didn't seem to mind, only wanting me to bring back presents.

I flew into Zurich because I had decided to take a train through the Alps to Milan. I missed seeing trees. Shortly after the journey began, the train went into a very long tunnel. A few minutes passed before we came out the other end. I was suddenly surrounded by spectacular mountains, vibrant with autumn-colored trees. I was overwhelmed by the beauty and started to cry. It had been so long since I had seen anything so wondrous.

When I returned to Israel, my passport was stamped with the work visa as promised.

CHAPTER TEN

Queen Dina

SHORTLY AFTER MY RETURN, I DECIDED TO GO TO JORDAN and ask Queen Dina if she would talk with me about her life. Although she had never spoken about it when I met her many years earlier, I had later learned that she had been prevented from seeing her child for seven years after her divorce from King Hussein. I had also been told about her courage—she had later fallen in love with and married the king's enemy, she and her new husband had formed a relationship with an Israeli journalist, and under her direction had pulled off the largest prisoner exchange in history.

But first I stopped in Bethlehem to visit her husband, Salah Tamari. Dina traveled between her homes in Bethlehem, Egypt, and Jordan, while Salah had become a minister in charge of monitoring illegal Israeli settlements in the West Bank. He had been a frequent guest at our home in Washington, but I had not seen him since the peace signing three years earlier. For reasons I didn't understand, he and Marwan were not on the best of terms, but Salah and I had remained friendly.

I arrived in Bethlehem and looked for Salah's office building. The signs were in Arabic, and I walked in and out of his building several times, thinking I must have the wrong address. There were bullet-ridden and partially missing walls, covered with graffiti, just like my office at the TV station. Once I reached the third floor, I saw a simple wooden door decorated with a large Che Guevara–style headshot of Salah, his handsome face framed by a tilted green beret. This was the office of a queen's husband? I entered a small reception area decorated with white plastic chairs and was offered the customary Turkish coffee. Salah would be there momentarily, I was told. He arrived shortly afterward accompanied by a few guards. He greeted me warmly and invited me into his office. The decor was consistent: an old desk, two tattered love seats, a few more white plastic chairs.

His words made up for the lack of ambience. He had a compelling, almost mesmerizing way of quoting philosophers and writers. John LeCarré had once described Salah as "almost too handsome, sculpting words with his strong hands, always quoting, always quotable." It was true.

He told me about seeing Dina for the first time. She was passing through Bethlehem in her royal procession. He was fourteen years old, and she was in her late twenties. Salah and his friends were standing in Manger Square, near Christ's birthplace. "When her procession came toward my friends and me, we were pushed away by her security, which I hated and felt was unjust. I always remembered her like a Medusa with snakes coming out of her head, I remembered a creature whose presence deprived me of my presence," he said.

Years later, in London, he saw her again. "I couldn't believe the woman I was meeting was the same woman I had carried in my mind as the Medusa. In the myth of Medusa, she turns everyone she looks at into stone. Quite the opposite happened. She brought me to life, turned me into a human being." Salah described her as a woman with both moral and physical fortitude. She drove through blockades, walked through battlefields, stood up to a king, and went against the political direction of her country to make a public statement. "She is a woman of principle. When she believes in something she fights for it no matter what the challenges are. She is a steel fist in a velvet glove."

After our talk, Salah invited me for dinner at his home. We were driven up and over mountains, high above the troubled land, far removed from the conflict and strife below. It wasn't yet dark, but stars and a full moon were bright in the sky. Occasionally we came upon a shepherd and stopped while he crossed the road with his sheep.

Salah's house was a castle built out of stones. People from the villages had carried the stones to this piece of land over the years and slowly built this structure for Queen Dina. The interior was simple. Cushions were laid on wood furniture along the periphery. Books were plentiful. Outside of his few aides, there was no indication of civilization in sight. This was his sanctuary with Dina.

I went on to Jordan the next day, traveling through Jericho. Signs reminded me that Jericho, a 10,000-year-old town, was at one of the lowest elevations on earth, about 800 feet below sea level. Camels roamed freely, and crevasses in the mountains led to hidden monasteries. Although it was rich with biblical history, what engaged my imagination were images of Cleopatra being carried by her servants through these deserts from Egypt to visit her summer palace in Jericho. It had been almost fifteen years since I had first seen Queen Dina on a pay phone in a Washington, D.C., hotel lobby. Now I stood on a noisy street in Jordan pressing the receiver of a public phone to my ear. As I strained to hear the ringing on the other end, a woman answered. She asked me to hold on for "Her Highness." Finally, Dina came on the line. Salah had told her I was coming, and she'd expected my call. She offered to send her driver to the hotel the next day to take me to her home.

I waited outside my hotel and watched a large Mercedes driven by a man in a military uniform drive up at noon sharp. A short ride through Jordan took us past the royal palace. It had been just six months since the death of His Majesty King Hussein. Billboards of the next king and queen were going up with all the flurry of a new cigarette advertising campaign.

We came to a quiet street lined with apartment buildings. We slowed to a stop in a driveway and were met by two soldiers wearing perfectly ironed uniforms and berets. I walked up a flight of wide stairs and came to a set of large double wooden doors, the guards never more than a step behind me. A Sudanese housekeeper, Saidi, answered the door and quickly told me she had met Marwan in Tunisia and that she had been a big fan of his when he was a soccer player. She led me into a large living room that was furnished 1960s style: cream-colored chairs, a sofa with a large floral pattern, and a green shag rug. There were several Whistler-style portraits of Queen Dina wearing her tiara and portraits of her daughter, Princess Alia.

I was seated and served tea. Several minutes later, Queen Dina entered the living room looking aged but beautiful. At seventy-five her hair was swept up in a french twist above her frail face, and she wore a floral print summer dress and high heels. She was the same humble, shy beauty with perfect English manners whom

I'd remembered. Apologizing for keeping me waiting, she explained that her cat was giving birth on the patio. She walked to the couch carrying a huge Coco Chanel tote bag, which she hugged on her lap throughout our entire three-hour visit.

I told her about my experience of losing custody of my children. She was reluctant to discuss her personal life, but she told me that she had some old photographs and asked if I would be interested in seeing them. She excused herself, and after ten minutes she returned with a white plastic bag, which she said she'd found at the bottom of a closet. The bag was full of black-and-white photos of her royal wedding, discarded like an old pair of shoes. She laid out the photos on the coffee table, worrying the whole time that she was boring me. She never once spoke about her experience that day, except to say it was her duty.

When I returned the following month to interview her, on my way back to Jordan, at the Allenby Bridge between Jericho and the Jordan River the car was meticulously checked for explosives. An Israeli soldier tapped on my window as I sat in the backseat. I rolled the window down and the soldier asked why I was going to Jordan. I told him I was going to visit Queen Dina. After more probing about the nature of my visit, the soldier finally broke into a smile and said, "Queen Dina! Now *that* is a real queen!" I smiled in agreement, and we drove away.

After an hour of proper tea and gentle reassurances, she started opening up. As a child growing up in the family palace in Alexandria, she was intrigued by a man who came to their garden carrying a sack of homemade soaps on his back. He was invited to have tea with her and her mother. He had been born in Nablus, a town in Palestine. His colorful tales and his descriptions of biblical towns stirred her imagination. "My family made me aware that he was no longer in his home or his country, but he represented his land. If someone had asked me to draw Palestine, I would have drawn this man. I felt I belonged to his land, to all the lands," she said. She imagined that any land that could create such a gentle, worthy man was where she wanted to belong.

Saidi walked in and out of the room to check on us, eventually joining Dina on the couch. Dina explained that Saidi had been her friend from childhood. Saidi's father had been bought on the slave market many years before and was saved by Dina's family when they bought him. Dina's family treated the young girl like part of an extended family and valued her service to them. Sixty-five years later, they remained loyal friends. Dina's world may have seemed limited within the palace gates as a child, but her friendship with Saidi and the colorful storyteller widened her horizons. They led her to her life's passion: unity in the Middle East and the disappearance of class differences.

Dina had first met her third cousin, Hussein, when she was twelve years old. Both born into the Hashemite family, their relatives ruled a vast portion of the Middle East. Dina's cousins sat on thrones, and her aunts had royal processions in Saudi Arabia, Egypt, and Iraq. Her childhood consisted of family visits to relatives' palaces, which was how she had first met the slightly younger prince of Jordan at a family gathering in London.

They were reintroduced after she graduated from Cambridge University in 1953, where she had studied the romantic poets Keats and Shelley. Hussein, newly crowned as king, was interested in marriage, and she was interested in pursuing a career of writing and teaching. After a few brief meetings at which both of their families were present, the king said to Dina's father, "By your permission, I intend to propose to my cousin."

Dina's father was ready to support Dina in any choice she made. "I told His Majesty that I wanted to wait before I married," Dina told me. "I had goals I wanted to accomplish." She wasn't interested in marrying him or anyone else at the time, and it did not seem she had any plans to marry him in the future either. But the king disregarded her answer and announced their wedding to President Nasser of Egypt while on a visit about two weeks later. News of a wedding spread rapidly throughout the Middle East. Ruling families were calling to offer their congratulations. Not wanting to bring embarrassment to her family, Dina agreed to the marriage. "He announced it, so there was nothing I could do. I wanted to write. I wanted to have a career before getting involved in family affairs or matrimony." Dina had been brought up to choose her own way. "I was committing myself to a life I never visualized. I thought I was going to be a single, independent woman in control of my own life," she said.

Dina was received warmly by the Jordanians. They gathered in the streets to welcome her and celebrate her marriage on April 18, 1955. She said it was very grand, and the attention was a bit embarrassing. She got along well with the king and did what was expected of her: going on official visits, attending cultural activities in schools, making appearances at hospitals. But she wanted more: "I always wanted to contribute something to Arabs. I believed in Arab unity and I thought my beliefs were in line with the king's," she said. Dina's values and views were known to the Jordanians, making her immensely popular—perhaps too popular.

Dina knew that the king's mother, Queen Zein, a formidable woman whom Dina didn't like to speak about, was creating tension at the palace. Dina was asked to stop having speaking engagements and appearing in public. Dina was frustrated but struggled to keep her marriage strong. She gave birth to their first and only child, Princess Alia, in 1956. "Everyone thought we would name our child Princess Zein after the king's mother. Instead I chose the name Alia after Queen Alia of Iraq. She was magnificent. His Majesty was wonderful about letting me choose. He had great sensitivity and understanding."

When Alia was eight months old, Dina's father was in a car accident in Egypt. She was encouraged by Queen Zein to travel to Cairo to see him. Dina didn't want to leave Alia, but the queen mother reassured her that Alia would be fine. Dina felt comfortable knowing that Mrs. Graig, a British nanny she had hired to watch over Alia, would be there. After visiting with her father for a week, she was getting ready to leave when a call came from the king telling her that she should not return. He said there were some problems and that he would let her know when she could return. It seemed Queen Zein had pressured the king to divorce Dina, not granting permission for her to reenter the country or see her daughter. Her citizenship didn't matter. "This came as a shock. I would have never left if I had known I'd be prevented from returning. I didn't come back because I kept being told never mind, spend another week, and this just got carried on like that."

"Who told you?" I asked.

"The person responsible."

"The king?"

She nodded.

"I had no idea why this was happening. Absolutely no idea. Divorce papers were sent to me."

Nearly a year passed with little communication from the king and no contact with her daughter. Dina's uncle intervened and insisted that Dina see the child. Due to his pressure, it was arranged for Dina to see Princess Alia in Turkey. She traveled there with her uncle, the prince regent, and was met by Queen Zein and Mrs. Graig. They stayed at the royal palace in Turkey, where Dina was refused any private time with her daughter. The queen mother was present throughout the short visit but would not discuss the situation with Dina. "Prince Regent swears that when she saw me, she said, 'Mama.'" In a somber voice Dina describes this as a miracle.

Dina believed that this was thanks to Mrs. Graig, who vowed to keep her memory alive. But the two women agreed not to communicate after parting ways, because Dina did not want to jeopardize Mrs. Graig's position. "It was more important to me that I knew Mrs. Graig was with her and that she would remind Alia of me. I always knew I would be reunited with my daughter. I just didn't know when."

For the next six years, Dina lived between Egypt and London and was continuously denied contact with her daughter. Information about Princess Alia came from newspapers and letters from friends. "I thanked God for my blessings instead and prayed for a resolution instead of focusing on the negative side," she said.

The king eventually remarried, this time to the daughter of a British army officer who was stationed in Jordan. After his new marriage, Dina was no longer seen as a threat, and the king paid her a visit.

Dina happened to be at a London hospital, undergoing surgery, when the king asked to see her. "The family doctor, an Englishman, came and said, 'I have a message for you. His Majesty the king would like to come visit you.'"

Initially she refused, but after days of requests, she finally relented.

"He came in very sweetly and asked if I would forgive him. I said, 'Yes, but what about Alia, whom I haven't seen in years now?' He said, 'I'll arrange that as soon as possible.'"

It took another six months before a meeting was arranged.

She traveled again with her uncle the prince regent, to the old Amman airport. "We were standing in a little room where dignitaries are met, and a second later somebody came through the door. It was His Majesty, holding onto Alia's hand. She immediately let go of him and hugged me. That was the other great miracle of my life. I am sure it was something completely natural. No one told her to do that. It was one of God's great blessings." Dina's relationship with Alia strengthened over the next few years, and they spent more and more time together. She took many subsequent trips to Jordan but never fully understood what had happened.

In 1967, when Alia turned eleven, Jordan entered a phase of political instability. The war between Palestinians and Israelis caused an influx of Palestinian refugees into Jordan. The Palestinians continued waging war from inside the refugee camps in Jordan. Israel was threatening to attack Jordan if the king could not control the Palestinians. Dina had great sympathy for the Palestinian people and still dreamed of a united Arab world.

As tension grew between King Hussein's government and the Palestinians, a battle broke out between them in 1968 that came to be known as the Battle of Karameh. The unmovable force of Palestinians was led by a dashing young commando, Salah Tamari. Jordan was defeated in the battle, and they were unsuccessful in capturing Tamari.

Several months after the battle, Tamari traveled to England. Dina was also in England, and mutual friends asked if they would like to meet at an exhibit of Palestinian art. Dina was eager to meet this young leader to get a balanced view of all sides of the conflict. Tamari, however, was not interested in meeting anyone from the royal family. Nevertheless, under pressure from his friends, he finally agreed to the introduction. It was a meeting that shook their worlds. By the end of the evening, Salah had proposed.

"He was exceptional and outspoken and, at the same time, shy. I admired how much he was committed to his cause. We had the same visions of unity."

Salah was twenty-four at the time, and Dina was thirty-nine.

"Salah stayed on for a few more days and then"—in Dina's formal wording—"feelings came to be. I was going to see His

Majesty who was also in London, and I felt he should know of our feelings for each other. I found telling him difficult, but he gave me his blessing.

"I felt I had a duty to tell my family as well. I wasn't going to ask their permission to have a relationship with Salah, but I didn't want to upset anyone within reason. I thought he was such a worthy and unusual person, the kind of person I could respect very much. We had things in common. There wasn't anything that felt strange to me at all. Other people might have thought, What is happening? But to me it was normal."

Salah had told me something similar: "Maybe she touched a very special chord in me. It was like a reflex that I proposed marriage after a few hours of knowing her. Sometimes it doesn't take more than a few seconds to connect with someone. It just demeans it to analyze it. The proposal wasn't conventional, but neither was the answer, and neither was the eventual marriage."

Dina did not want to marry right away, so Salah visited her over the next year in London and in Egypt. The situation in Jordan became increasingly tense, and a civil war was brewing between the Palestinians and the king. Salah was still leading his Palestinian forces, under the direction of Arafat and Abu Jihad. Dina made frequent trips to Jordan to talk to the king because she thought that she could help bridge the gap between the two sides.

"I thought that perhaps I could help smooth over the differences. I hoped I could throw cold water on some of the embers. Then there was an escalation in the hostilities. I arrived in Jordan to visit my daughter, and things were so tense at the airport that I was flown up to the palace in a helicopter."

Dina tried talking to the king again, asking for his mercy, to please not attack the Palestinians. She left the palace and went to see Salah before leaving the country. Within several hours of her departure, the king attacked. This was the beginning of what came to be known as "Black September" when thousands of Palestinians were killed.

"Black September was illogical. There was bleeding and chaos, misunderstanding and hatred. In a manner of speaking," Dina said, "the king ordered the death of the man I love."

Dina feared Salah could be killed and decided that they should get married. She wanted to make a statement to the king and the Arab world at large. She wanted her love for Salah to set an example for Arab unity.

"It was a nightmare. I set off to return to Jordan to find him. I wanted to get a message to him that I wanted to marry him right away. Our relationship could have been a bridge, a glimpse of hope in a turbulent time."

Salah had told me, "We got married during Black September. We had no communication for several days. Dina had incredible courage, and she wanted to be near me. She took a single-engine propeller helicopter with a pilot in training. I would never do it, but she did it. She came to the front lines in disguise to find me. She knew who could lead her to me. There were roadblocks and I was sort of 'wanted,' so I had to move around. It's not easy in the middle of a war. I was in Amman, in the al Hussein Refugee Camp. I had received the message and I was sitting with Abu Jihad. I didn't want to get married against the will of my leadership, so I was about to ask for his permission.

"A bomb exploded over our heads, the second floor collapsed, and everyone started running. When the smoke cleared, I was smiling. Abu Jihad asked, 'What are you smiling about?' I said, 'Well, I want to get married.' He said, 'NOW?! How can you think of marriage?' But then he said, 'Okay, get married!' And that was it.

"Dina and I found each other, and I went for a religious sheik. The first two sheiks changed their minds when they saw Dina.

They recognized her, although she was in disguise, and they were afraid to perform the ceremony. The next day we sent someone to find a sheik. We didn't tell them who was getting married. When he arrived at our hiding place, several people were sitting around with guns. It was dark, and gunfire was all around us. The sheik was scared, so he married us. I wanted to give him money. He said, 'No, I don't want money. Just don't tell anyone that I made this marriage or that I saw you or you saw me.'

"The next day she left the camp. We stirred the waters of our society in many ways. Many people found it unbelievable, maybe out of jealousy. I thought it was a simple story. I was a man; she a woman; we fell in love. Very simple."

It was several months before they saw each other again, this time in Lebanon, where they rented a two-room house in the town of Sidon.

I asked Dina what she expected her day-to-day life to be like with Salah. She said she never thought about it. She was prepared to have a little home in the valley, a one-room house. "It was total commitment," she said. "Who wants a palace? A palace is an idea. One respects a palace because of what it stands for—the people who should be doing the right thing, steering the wheel of a nation, of a country. So it has a certain respect in one's mind. But it has nothing to do with comfort or fairy tales."

Through the years, she still loved the king as her cousin, as a man who became her friend. At the time of our visit, she was still saddened by his recent death and was spending time in Jordan to be near her daughter.

Dina was still romantic about her life with Salah. "We are like Odysseus and Penelope," she said. "He could never get home; the winds would always take him in another direction."

Dina and Salah lived simply and happily for the next eleven years. Their home in south Lebanon was open to all, constantly welcoming visitors: Druze, Christian, and Muslim. Together they read and studied mythology, passing time in front of their fireplace.

Then in 1982, Lebanon was invaded by Israel. During an incursion into their village, all the men were required to turn themselves in, and they were taken to prison. Salah resisted, hiding, moving from location to location, eventually ending up in a church. He finally turned himself in because he didn't want to endanger the lives of those protecting him. He was in prison for eighteen months.

The Israelis soon realized they were holding the highest-ranking PLO member ever to be captured. The guards were quite taken with his eccentric personality and finely tuned intellect. A commander suggested that they bring one of Israel's renowned journalists to interview him. During the interview, the two men became intrigued by each other. They found themselves discussing T. S. Eliot, crossing the line between captive and captor. Salah asked that the journalist contact Dina and let her know he was alive. He told him to use the code name Penelope so she knew it was an authentic message.

So impressed was the journalist with Salah that he spoke to his government and suggested they let Salah out of prison from time to time under his supervision. The writer wanted to introduce Salah to other writers, philosophers, and families from Israel. The government agreed to occasional outings and also gave Dina permission to see him during these excursions. Salah was taken from the Ansar prison camp blindfolded and handcuffed because none of the prisoners knew the location of the camp. Dina was given a disguise and fake passport by the Israelis to enter Israel. She would stay with Salah at the home of the Israeli journalist and his wife. During these brief visits, a close friendship began to grow between the journalist, his wife, Dina, and Salah.

Wanting to repay the journalist for his efforts, Dina took a trip into remote parts of Lebanon to track down faction leaders possibly holding Israeli soldiers as prisoners. She thought she could let their families know they were safe in the same way that she now knew about Salah's condition. She discovered that there were six young men being held in a house high up in the mountains. The Israeli government thought these six soldiers were dead. Dina got permission from the faction leaders to visit the men. She had to take a dangerous trip into the mountains at night for her visit. Hiding a tape recorder under her coat, she secretly taped the men. After returning with evidence in hand, she asked the Israeli journalist to arrange a meeting for her with his government. Everything had to be top secret. She could not be seen meeting with the Israeli government. Again they sent her several disguises and had her travel through three different countries, changing disguises in each one, until they met in a hotel room in London. She presented the tapes, proof that the soldiers were alive.

On her next visit with Salah, he recommended proposing a prisoner exchange. She began negotiations and through her efforts, involving months of work, she oversaw the largest prisoner exchange ever to take place in the Middle East. In exchange for these 6 Israeli soldiers, 8,000 Palestinians were released.

After all her work, a ceremony was planned for the release of prisoners in Algeria. Several governments donated planes to take some of the Palestinian prisoners to Algeria for the ceremony. Salah would be the main speaker, and Dina and Salah would be reunited. She waited in Geneva with other Arab leaders, and together they would fly to Algiers. Dina had gone to her hotel to rest, and to her surprise all the male leaders left for Algeria without her.

"Quite chauvinistic, don't you think?" she asked me.

"What did you do?"

"I just caught the next plane."

By the time Dina arrived, she had missed Salah's speech, and he had been moved up north to an army base with several hundred freed prisoners and their families. Dina was driven to the facility. She stood watching the prisoners reunite with wives and children. Her eyes searched for Salah. Then suddenly, directly behind her, was Salah standing with his arms wide open and a huge smile on his face.

To this day, some of these Israeli prisoners still visit her with their families in Egypt.

I stopped at the palace of Princess Alia, Dina's daughter, before leaving Jordan. Alia was warm and humble like her mother and a bit more outgoing. I asked her about her early years of separation from her mother. Dina's intuition had been right: hiring Mrs. Graig as Alia's nanny when she was a baby had kept Dina's memory alive. Mrs. Graig had helped Alia to imagine her mother on great adventures and never doubted that she would eventually return. Mrs. Graig had stayed with Alia and became the nanny to her children as well.

Alia said that growing up with Dina during her teenage years was like coming of age in a spy movie. Her mother would tell her she was going on a secret mission to meet the opposition. She would put a pistol in her Chanel purse and sneak off in a car. Alia had to cover for her, informing the guards of her mother's whereabouts only if she didn't return by a certain time. Alia told me that Dina was a very good shot.

I was comforted knowing that although Alia had been separated from her mother, she still had a deep admiration for her. I hoped that one day my children would be just as proud of me.

CHAPTER ELEVEN

The Peacemakers

WHEN I RETURNED TO RAMALLAH, I WAS STILL UPSET with Marwan, but if I focused on this anger, I knew it would rub off on my children. I was still able to see them daily and, like Queen Dina, I wanted to focus on my opportunities rather than my restrictions. After I had been there about a year and Marwan's work demanded that he travel often, the children began asking him if I could sleep over on occasion when he was away. Otherwise they would have been left with his housekeeper and guards, all of whom spoke little English.

On one of my first nights there, someone came to the door. Looking through the security hole, I could see no one; it was pitch black. I called the guards downstairs, who said no one had entered the building. Several minutes later they knocked at the door and entered quickly with guns drawn. Before I could finish telling them what happened, they told us to stay inside with the door locked. After about fifteen minutes they returned with an elderly lady from downstairs. While searching for the mysterious visitor, they knocked on everybody's doors, guns still drawn. They discovered that our neighbor from downstairs had come up and knocked on the door to invite us for brunch the next day. We apologized and, of course, graciously accepted.

Sometimes when I stayed over, the children invited two of their closest friends from school to join them. One was a girl Deena's age, and the other, a boy, was younger than Tarik. I was fascinated watching them play. They took Marwan's large apartment and turned it into a miniature city. They created stores, a real estate office, a bank, a psychologist's office, and asked many questions about how the world functioned, such as, "How do you rent an apartment? How do you open a bank account?" The one area that they developed on their own, without any help, was a "human rights office." When someone misbehaved, he or she was sent to a room for solitary confinement. If the defendant complained about meals, then one of the children acted as the attorney and went to the human rights office to complain. I watched in amazement. They had incorporated topics into their play that I had grasped only in adulthood.

One of the most inspiring experiences that I had was meeting peacemakers—not elected or appointed officials but true peacemakers, citizens taking peace into their own hands. These people seldom made the news. I sometimes received frantic cell phone calls from friends in the States who had just seen footage of an "uprising" or conflict in Ramallah. I would stand on my terrace, which overlooked the city, and report back that it was calm and peaceful. It took me awhile to understand that any activity whatsoever was often exaggerated by the media. If I hadn't been living there, I never would have known about the many Israelis and Palestinians who were reaching out to one another.

My own country was actively participating as well. President Clinton was standing by the peace agreement he had brokered and supported. There was great excitement among the Palestinians that President Clinton was coming for a visit, scheduled for December 1998. This visit solidified his commitment to bring opportunities to the people and his recognition of the Palestinians, not as refugees but as legitimate people with a government and a nationhood. Commerce Secretary William Daley, who was accompanying the Clintons on their trip, held a briefing at the Brookings Institution, a Washington, D.C., think tank. He spoke about what they hoped to accomplish on the trip, their interest in building a Palestinian economy and dismantling stumbling blocks such as closures and holdbacks at checkpoints. He wanted the economy to include development of an industrial zone in Gaza, a healthy import and export community, jobs for the new middle class. All of this would be made possible by donor countries that pledged money to support these efforts.

By the time President and Mrs. Clinton, along with Secretary Daley, arrived, advance teams had been in the Gaza Strip distributing American flags. I went to witness the events firsthand. Palestinians waved the flags enthusiastically while the sound of honking horns, symbolic of their appreciation, filled the streets. There was hope in the air. Clinton made an encouraging address to President Arafat and the Palestinian Legislative Council: "We must believe that everyone can win in the Middle East," he said. He recognized their "pains, losses suffered from violence, separation of families and restrictions of movement on people and goods." The country was electrified with promises of a new future, while he reminded them that they had the opportunity "to shape a new Palestinian future on their own land." I knew there were people who didn't support Clinton or Arafat or the Israelis. They didn't want compromise; they didn't want Israel to exist. But during that time, these people were a minority, unsupported by the masses. The peacemakers dominated the scene.

One of the great peacemakers I'd met was Dr. Fathi Arafat, Yasir's older brother. A friend invited me to attend a meeting held at the Palestinian Red Crescent Hospital in Ramallah. This was one of the hospitals that had been built by Dr. Arafat, and as with all the other hospitals he built, there was an art museum and theater attached, as well as rooms for social gatherings. In this facility, the social area was on the top floor. It was a large, open space that he had carefully designed using exposed wood, fireplaces, and comfortable chairs, plus a kitchen. Guests at his traditional midnight dinners were always well fed. (It is common to dine late in that part of the world—sometimes due to the climate, sometimes for privacy's sake, sometimes just for the novelty.) Each week he invited Israelis and Palestinians with similar interests to dine together. Everyone was eager to accept: scientists, doctors, teachers, artists, filmmakers, musicians. These dinners often marked the first time that many of the Israeli guests had ever ventured into an Arab town. As they shared ideas, people who had been perceived as enemies became human beings. These salons became well known for drawing idealists and skeptics alike. From these meetings, relationships blossomed.

I became friendly with an Israeli woman named Mari whom I met at one of the gatherings. She was having great success with a program that brought together small groups of Palestinian and Israeli students just before they were old enough to join their respective armies. They attended the gatherings with their parents and together they wrote their own "declaration of human rights." She told me she was holding about one session a week and was greatly impressed by the youths' ability to recognize one another's rights. In a small way, she was making a difference.

A few months after Fathi and I first met, he took me to his childhood home in Jerusalem, an ancient stone house in the center of the Old City. We entered the now-abandoned house and took a narrow stone staircase to the roof, where he and Yasir once played. From this vantage point, we could see the most cherished devotional sites of Christianity, Judaism, and Islam. The roof was situated like the axis of a wheel: in one direction was the sacred Wailing Wall. If you turned slightly, you saw the Dome of the Rock, from which Muhammad ascended. Turning a bit more, you overlooked the Holy Sepulcher, where Jesus was nailed to the cross. Dr. Arafat said that he and his brother had literally grown up able to see all sides.

He thought the current conflict had nothing to do with religion. To him, it was solely political. He spoke about his brother's marriage to Suha in the same terms. "He chose to marry Suha because he loved her," he said. "It didn't make a difference what religion she was." His decision to keep the marriage quiet was image related, not because he was afraid to show people he married someone from another religion, but because the men surrounding him demanded complete devotion. We climbed back down the wobbly stairs and picked some mint from a small garden before reentering the house.

Fathi opened a door on one side of what had been the family sitting room—a large space with high ceilings and large double doors at one end. When he opened the doors, the Islamic Art Museum was right there: the sitting room was directly connected to one of the large exhibit rooms. There were treasures of enormous proportion inside, sculptures and ornate etchings. This had molded his belief that we should live with art and appreciate its healing properties; it taught the value of expression and the power of vision.

On the way back home, I asked Fathi if, as children, he knew that his brother would be a leader one day.

"Yes, I knew when Yasir was five," he said.

"How?" I wondered.

"He told us. He announced it to the family, and he told us he would rebuild Palestine."

As kids, they had enjoyed building cities out of little cardboard boxes. Now Yasir was trying to build a nation, and Fathi was building hospitals.

Next to my own home in Ramallah was a nursery school run by a beautiful Muslim girl who was about twenty-two years old. Her parents were very religious, bordering on fundamentalist. I told her about Fathi's gatherings. She was interested but was afraid to attend in her own home town. What if her parents found out?

One evening close to Christmas, I drove into Jerusalem with her for dinner. She was curious about West Jerusalem, the Israeli side of the city. She had heard it was full of places for young people to gather, just like in the United States, and she wanted to meet Israelis her age. But it was unheard of for a Palestinian from the occupied territories to do such a thing, especially someone from such a religious family. Still, we went.

We walked into a crowded restaurant. There was a large table with about ten young Israelis sitting around, all engaged in lively conversation. With nowhere else to sit, I asked if we could use two empty chairs at the end of the table. They nodded, and we sat quietly for a few minutes, watching them. I began a conversation with several of the Israelis, and I could tell they were curious about my friend, so I introduced her. She told them her name and that she was a Palestinian living in Ramallah. Word quickly got around the table, and all eyes turned to my friend. The Israelis were initially surprised, but their curiosity quickly got the better of them. They were polite and asked questions about one another's lives, which, it turned out, were more similar than it appeared. They asked where the others lived, about their schooling, about their work, about TV and music. They didn't talk politics at all. The atmosphere was warm and promising, as well as sad. All it took to bring these young people together was a little effort, a few moments of discomfort. The formula for peace on a small scale was right in front of me.

This brightened my otherwise dismal mood. Marwan had taken the children skiing in Germany for Christmas, and I was left by myself. It was very lonely; Christmas had always been a big family celebration at home. Fortunately, I was invited by a former Arafat adviser and spokesman, Bassam Abu Sharif, to spend Christmas Eve attending mass at the Church of the Nativity, on the site where Christ was born. I went to Bethlehem hours before the mass to participate in a small tour with the mayor and the high priest of the church. Bethlehem lacked all the commercialism of the West. There were no Santa Clauses and reindeer decorations, but there were religious leaders from all over the world crowding into the town for the evening celebration.

I met my hosts at the church and was taken with several other invitees to the ruins of a city hidden underneath. In Bethlehem, there are literally layers of civilizations, ruins upon ruins buried atop one another. We entered this hidden city through an iron gate and eased our way down several sets of steep, uneven stone staircases into darkness. Several men who accompanied us lit candles, illuminating tiny cavelike rooms filled with children's skulls, hundreds of them. "When Herod ordered all boys under the age of two to be killed, looking for the Christ Child, the killings took place here," the priest explained. I was overwhelmed by the sight and couldn't help but notice that there were larger skulls scattered about as well. These were the skulls of the mothers who had refused to leave their sons.

I walked up the stairs, shaken, back into the Church of the Nativity. Back on street level, I walked over boards that were placed in such a way as to allow a glimpse of the Byzantine floors below, placed there in the year 327 A.D. under the direction of Helena, the mother of Constantine. And now I was in this simple church, with its great spirit, where people of peace gathered for prayer beneath this biblical town's starry Christmas sky.

Shortly after, I met Palestinian and Israeli parents who had come together to form an organization called the Parents Circle, which I'd learned about through a friend. Each had lost an immediate family member in the conflict, but instead of fighting, they said to each other, "Let's not meet at our graveyards. Let's gather and set a strong example for others. If we can forgive each other because we want a better life for our children, then anyone should be able to do so."

One of the mothers, Robi Damelin, is an Israeli whose twenty-seven-year-old son David had been killed by a Palestinian sniper. I met her with a Palestinian man whose brother had been killed by an Israeli soldier. He told me he was standing at the checkpoint with him waiting to go through, and a small argument broke out about his papers. Many Palestinians were watching. One Israeli soldier walked up and shot and killed him. The brother believed this was done just to scare the other Palestinians and teach them not to argue. He wept when he told me the story, and Robi consoled him.

Next she introduced me to a Palestinian woman, Nadwa, with whom she often traveled. "Sometimes I'm so filled with grief about the death of my son, I can't go on," Robi told me. "But then I feel Nadwa's hand in mine, and I have the strength to continue."

What was this internal process that allowed them to let go of their anger? I asked Robi. "Forgiveness," she said. "If you can truly experience it, it is magical." These people were showing me that forgiveness didn't alleviate their pain, but it helped them to react constructively.

There were those who did not believe the peace agreement (the Declaration of Principles) was fair, and therefore did not want to participate in reconciliation. They believed Arafat had given in to pressure and he should have gotten more. On the other side there were extremists who believed in their steadfast biblical ties to the land and fundamentalists who believed they were being called by a higher power for jihad. These people were contained after the peace signing, silenced by a larger voice of hope, but they still existed and tried to sabotage and punish those around them, whom they considered evil traitors. Those who yearned for peace had to express their feelings carefully. Some of the most educated and opened-minded Palestinians still couldn't bring themselves to join in. They would support peace, but they were reluctant to participate in face-to-face reconciliation.

I decided to produce a show for children called *Magic Glasses*, starring a large blind bunny who gave out magic glasses. When children put the glasses on, they gained new perspectives on the world. In one episode, a large bird with a broken wing complains about his injury, and the magic bunny explains we can all chip in to make the world better for ourselves and people around us, but it takes effort from everyone. The children sing as they look for branches to build a ladder for the bird who can't fly. The lyrics are about peace and everyone working together, to make friends out of enemies. It demonstrated how to respond to the same situation several different ways: anger could provoke violence, but it could also lead to dialogue.

I had a huge seven-foot bunny made by a puppeteer in Jordan. My crew couldn't cross the borders with me when it was time to bring the puppet back to Palestine, so I had to travel with this big bunny in several pieces. There was a ridiculous scene at the border between Jordan and Palestine when Israeli soldiers put the puppet on platforms to sweep it for bombs. My bunny made it through with me. Many of the actors from the television station, who were participating in their own reconciliation work, were eager to perform in the piece. Some of them told me that they had been in a theater program run by James Marrioni from New York University. He was their playwright-in-residence and had used theater for reconciliation projects in other parts of the world. He had been sent to the region as part of a reconciliation program that USAID supported. His assignment was to start the first Israeli-Palestinian-Jordanian theater group. The program had consisted of bringing Palestinian, Jordanian, and Israeli performers together in England for six weeks. They had participated in the program because they wanted acting experience; no one believed they would develop relationships with the people coming from "the other side." They lived together and spent an intense six weeks getting to know each other. From this experience, they now supported peace and spoke to groups about the possibility and encouragement of reconciliation. Marrioni had written a play for them, *The Last Enemy*, about actors who wanted a stubborn old director to give their play a new ending and his refusal to do so. It was a brilliant work, in which Palestinian roles were played by Israelis and vice versa. In one graveyard scene, a Palestinian woman plays an Israeli mother who has lost a son, and an Israeli woman plays a Palestinian mother who has lost a son. After their six weeks in England, everyone had been profoundly changed. They now understood one another and realized they all wanted the same thing: to live in a peaceful world. They were anxious to introduce me to Marrioni the following month, knowing we'd have plenty in common.

I met Marrioni at the Grand Hotel in Ramallah. We discussed the possibility of having the Israeli and Palestinian actors perform their play in Ramallah and Gaza. The play had been performed at the United Nations, the Perez Center for Peace, and several other venues in the United States. Were the West Bank and Gaza ready for this? I said I would help.

I made an appointment with the minister of culture, Yasser Abed Rabbo. To my surprise, he was afraid of having direct contact with Marrioni because people opposed to the reconciliation efforts might threaten him or his family. So I had Marrioni in one room and the minister in another room, and I carried messages back and forth between them. The minister told me he supported and respected Marrioni's work, but it was still too early for him to allow the play to be performed in Ramallah. He felt people still needed time to acclimate themselves to the idea of living in peace among people whom they'd resented for so long. He told me we were rushing things.

On the way out of our meeting, I stopped by the office of a friend who worked at the culture ministry. I thought if I explained the situation to him, perhaps he could influence the minister. I asked if he would meet me for coffee later. We met that evening, and I told him about the wonderful work that Marrioni was doing. To my surprise, he told me that he didn't think he could support the play. Like the minister, he said that people had to experience forgiveness in their own time.

"I want to show you something," he said as he lifted his shirt to show me deep, round scars on his stomach. "When I was a teenager, I lived in Gaza. Israel invaded and rounded up the boys from my village. I had holes burnt into my stomach with cigarettes while the soldiers demanded information about people whom I did not know. All the while, I recited national songs to myself, to help me endure the pain. This was senseless and unjustified. I cannot say, 'I forgive you; let's turn the page and move on.'"

I stopped pressuring him. I never tried to impose my peace on anyone else again.

Instead, I suggested that Marrioni come with me to visit Fathi Arafat in the Gaza Strip. Perhaps Arafat would support the play being performed there. This would be even riskier than Ramallah, however, because of its large Hamas population. We traveled to the border by taxi, and Fathi had a car waiting to take us to Khan Unis, a refugee camp at the far end of Gaza, where he had built what was known as the City of Hope. This refugee camp had once consisted of old, cracked buildings and poorly paved roads. There was little medical care, hope, or purpose in the lives of its inhabitants. Fathi had raised money for the Red Crescent to build a hospital. Instead of hiring a construction company from Jordan or another neighboring country, he enlisted the people of the refugee camp to build the hospital themselves, under the direction of several engineers. It would become their own: they would build it, work in it, and take pride in it.

The hospital started out small and quickly grew. It began to take over the camp as a museum was attached, then a center to make handicrafts, stores to sell the handicrafts, a school for the disabled, a computer center, a theater, a wedding hall with a kitchen, and a small furniture factory. The hospital itself looked like an art school, with paintings on all the walls and patients lying in their beds working on sculptures and crafts. A residential wing was being built for visiting doctors, social workers, psychologists, and artists, all of whom came to devote their time to this small miracle. Next came a cafeteria, where boys and girls could socialize. Fathi then built a secluded swimming pool for girls where they could wear swimsuits without feeling ashamed of their bodies, and he encouraged women to remove their veils. There were fundamentalists on the periphery, and several assassination attempts were made on Fathi's life because of his "liberal" ideas, but he felt no fear and proceeded unaffected by these threats.

There were many disabled orphans in this refugee camp. He bought them wheelchairs, and he adopted them, giving them his last name. (He also had two biological children, living in Cairo.) The children introduced themselves with great pride, happy to use his name. Adults felt the same. Fathi always had an entourage of at least twenty men; they served no immediate purpose but liked to be in close proximity to show their respect and be available in case an opportunity to show their gratitude arose.

We went to the theater that he had built. Marrioni was astonished by its construction, acoustics, magnificent velvet theater curtains, and the handicapped-accessible ramps for the wheelchairs. Fathi made sure that everyone was always included, and Marrioni was no exception. Fathi agreed to allow the play to be performed there.

He had arranged a dinner party for us that evening at his home in Gaza City. Getting back to Ramallah afterward was not an easy task, thanks to the checkpoints, and even more of a challenge since we could not leave his dinner until very late. Fathi had arranged for a car to take us to the edge of Gaza and then for another car to pick us up on the other side of no-man's-land at the Israeli border. Marrioni and I walked through no-man's-land at about 1:00 A.M. The soldiers there told us that one of our papers lacked a stamp we needed and that we had to walk all the way back to our starting point. Marrioni began to engage in a heated argument with the machine gun–wielding soldiers, completely fearless. Finally, I persuaded him to walk back with me and get the paper stamped.

When we returned to the border about an hour later and were allowed to pass through, we had to hope that a car would still be waiting for us. In the distance, I saw an old white automobile. As we approached, its stench—something akin to sheep—became almost unbearable. Now Marrioni had to persuade *me* to get into the car, as there was no other alternative. I finally agreed, laughing as Marrioni joked about the smell.

The driver was Arab and spoke Arabic and Hebrew but virtually no English. About an hour into the drive, high in the pitch-black mountains, we were stopped at another checkpoint. We sat in the car while soldiers shined flashlights in our faces and spoke with the driver in Hebrew. We were silent. The soldiers then asked us if we spoke English. Annoyed and tired, we said that we did. The soldiers, now glaring at us, asked for our passports. We handed them over. They surrounded our car, clutching their guns, while several of the other officers radioed people. Finally they got us out of the car and began asking us why we had American passports if we were Russian. It seems the driver didn't have a permit to drive a taxi, so he had told the soldiers, in Hebrew, that we were his friends. They asked him where we were from, and not knowing us and not knowing what to say, he had replied that we were Russians—and, in the minds of the Israelis, Russians with stolen passports. Once we resolved the situation, we were sent on our way. All in all, it was a four-hour adventure.

Fathi had a good relationship with his brother but did not want to be part of the new government or involved in any government bureaucracy. He told me that Arafat had asked him to be minister of health, and Fathi replied, "No! I couldn't bear to be stuck inside at meetings all day."

Marwan, not surprisingly, was extremely irritated by my friendships and activities. I called the children from Fathi's office one day, and Marwan answered. Fathi was sitting next to me, and

I told Marwan where I was and asked if he wanted to say hello. Marwan refused. Fathi could hear him, and I was embarrassed. I didn't know what to say to Fathi when I hung up. "Well, that's Marwan," he said, and we both laughed it off.

Fathi was eager to bring me into the fold. Often he would say to me, "I know there is something we are supposed to do together for peace, and one day we will find out what it is. It hasn't been revealed yet." In July 1999 he invited me on a week-long trip to Egypt to show me the Red Crescent hospitals he had built there as well. He told me we would have a pleasant drive through the Sinai and then take the ferry across the Suez Canal. "It's a relaxing drive," he assured me.

The drive, however, took seven hours and involved countless checkpoints: some Israeli, some Egyptian, some installed by the U.N. At the larger checkpoints, we were taken into a room for visitors, greeted by the person in charge, and given tea. Fathi was always given a warm welcome, and he rewarded everyone with his big, bright smile. Meanwhile, camels roamed, bedouins lolled in their colorful tents, and Fathi passed the time joking about his brother's less than classically handsome looks. (He couldn't help but admit that he and his brother looked very much alike.)

The long car ride gave us plenty of time to talk. I didn't know much about Fathi's family save for his brother, so I asked him about his wife, if she had known about his involvement with the Palestinian movement when she met him more than thirty years earlier in Cairo. "I only told her that I was tied to a revolution," he said. She didn't know much more, and neither did anyone else. Everything was done in secret. In the 1950s, initiation into Fatah was almost fraternal. No one knew who the other members were or who the leader was. If someone was perceived as a good candidate, he would be approached by a Fatah member. If the candidate expressed interest, then two Fatah members would be sent to observe him for a few months, monitoring how he functioned under pressure and assessing his level of dedication. Fathi had passed their tests.

Eventually the time came to reveal the leader and other members to one another, so Fathi was instructed to go to Kuwait and stay at a hotel popular among Palestinians. While there, he would be told about a meeting in which the elusive leader would be announced. Shortly after arriving in Kuwait, he ran into his brother at the hotel. Both claimed to be there on business and planned on having dinner with friends that evening.

Fathi received a message to go to a certain location at midnight. He slipped out of the hotel, hoping to avoid his brother. When he arrived for the meeting, he was met by his recruiters and escorted into the meeting room. And there was Yasir, leader of the Palestinians and the founder of the Fatah movement. Fathi was shocked: "From that night forward, I addressed him as my leader, not my brother."

As we approached the Suez Canal, cars were backed up for two miles waiting to cross. It was terribly hot. People had abandoned their cars and were guzzling water. A police car arrived and escorted us to the front, where we crossed on a floating bridge. I felt a bit embarrassed by the special treatment, but I was relieved to avoid the sweltering heat.

Fathi took me to an apartment building in a beautiful part of Cairo next to the Red Crescent. He installed me in a large guest apartment with a staff. He kept an apartment on another floor, where he entertained.

Fathi always had several agendas. A man whom I had met in Ramallah came to see us. He was handsome and had received a doctorate in engineering from UCLA. Fathi had wanted him to move to Ramallah to build a hospital for him, but the man was reluctant to leave his mother, aunts, and sisters in Cairo. Especially since his father had died, he felt he needed to be head of the household. I realized that in addition to Fathi's friendly invitation, he had hoped that perhaps I would develop an interest in this man and ask that he return to Ramallah with us—and therefore build Fathi's new hospital. Fathi must have indicated to the man that I was interested in marriage, because we were invited to the man's home for dinner that evening and every aunt, uncle, and cousin was there to meet me. As I realized what was going on, I greeted everyone and glared at Fathi (who sat sheepishly in a corner) between introductions.

Fathi asked the man to be my escort during my week-long stay in Cairo. This seemed harmless enough, if a bit funny. I went to a wedding with him that was great fun, especially watching the bride being led by belly dancers and men in traditional dress playing hand drums. The wedding started about midnight, just like Fathi's dinners. A few of the people seated at my table suggested that I take a horseback ride past the pyramids. I hadn't seen them yet, and it seemed like a wonderful idea to go right then in the middle of the night. I asked my host if we could take the hour drive to Giza and see if we could find horses to ride. He was reluctant, citing several reasons why it wasn't a good idea, but I was insistent and he finally agreed.

We stopped at the apartment where I was staying so I could change into pants, and then we drove for about an hour down a straight road that eventually dissolved into sand. I got out of the car and stared into the darkness, trying to see the pyramids. My new friend kept insisting that they were right in front of me and I finally realized that what I thought was the sky *were* the pyramids. We walked a bit and found a shepherd down a dirt road who had some horses. By this time, it was almost two in the morning. My escort, who had been boasting of his black belt, skydiving, parasailing, and other daring activities, admitted that he was afraid of horses. I told him that he could wait in the car and I would ride by myself. He refused, of course, and climbed on one of the horses, with much trepidation.

Accompanied by the shepherd, we wended our way through an ancient village to reach a path that would take us to the pyramids. The village was full of night owls: they slept during the day because of the heat and stayed awake during the cooler evenings. There were no cars, only dirt roads filled with wandering camels. People lined the paths, smoking water pipes and playing music. This scene, with the pyramids looming, was one of the most spectacular visions of my life. When we reached the open land surrounding the pyramids, I let my horse take off while the men stayed behind.

I was resting in my guest apartment several nights later before getting ready for dinner when Fathi called and said that he had a Jewish journalist and his wife in his apartment and wanted me to come down for a cocktail and meet them. They were going to be moving to Ramallah, and Fathi wanted me to smooth the way for them. I went to Fathi's apartment, and the couple asked me about various people they wanted to meet. Fathi had excused himself to take a phone call. When he returned, he began shooting me looks and tried to hurry me along. I said goodnight and went back to my apartment, suspicious.

Shortly afterward, there was a knock at the door. It was the maid from Fathi's apartment. She held a silver tray with a small, folded piece of paper. It was a note from Fathi saying that the phone call he had received while I was speaking to the couple was someone informing him that they were from the Mossad.

We left a couple of days later, picking up Fathi's sister's son, Nasser al Kidwa, the Palestinian ambassador to the United Nations, on the way. Riding home, listening to the Arabic radio station crackling in the background, I made out the name "John F. Kennedy Junior." I asked Fathi to translate. Kennedy's plane was missing off Martha's Vineyard. I went numb, thinking about this icon of *my* culture thousands of miles away. I suddenly longed for my own culture. As we made our way back to Ramallah, I looked forward to returning to the States soon.

CHAPTER TWELVE

Toujan al-Faisal

ALTHOUGH HE ALWAYS HAD CONCERNS ABOUT SECURITY, to my surprise Marwan permitted me to take a trip with the children to Jericho. He was traveling, and my children had asked if we could take the day trip together. To my surprise, he agreed. Of course, his car and staff took us. On the way, the driver pointed out what looked like a speck at the bottom of a deep valley in the desert. The mountains that surrounded us looked like rocks. He explained it was a small monastery that had been built by the Greek Orthodox and was sequestered where it was so that they could practice their faith without being attacked. He told me there was a walking path that took well over an hour, open to visitors wanting to visit the monastery. I wanted to take the walk, as did Tarik.

We drove closer and parked at the top of the entrance, along with other visitor cars. Deena wanted to stay with the driver in the little welcoming area and read her new *Archie* comics. I tried to convince her not to miss the opportunity, but she refused. She looked like a typical American teenager as I glanced back at her sitting on a chair, feet up on a table, reading her comic. I could see that she was still connected to her American culture. Tarik and I climbed down in the heat. When we finally arrived, a Greek Orthodox priest told me I couldn't enter because my sleeves were short and my arms were exposed. They believed this was disrespectful. I had left my light jacket in the car, anticipating the heat. A gentleman nearby had an extra jacket and offered it to me, allowing me to enter.

The tiny monastery, only four rooms, was filled with iconic treasures. In the last room we entered was a glass coffin holding the skeleton of a priest, dressed in his cloak and even his old worn-out shoes. I was fascinated by this, but Tarik, now eleven years old, was frightened, so we climbed back up, and made the remaining hour-long trip to Jericho.

We went to the only large resort, complete with a two-story restaurant and a huge shopping area, featuring products from the Dead Sea. When we sat to eat, Deena and Tarik told me that the place was owned by a couple they referred to as "Aunt and Uncle," friends of Marwan. We asked the waiter if they were there. When they came to the table and recognized the children, they sent a feast over and refused to let me pay anything for it. After a wonderful afternoon, the kind that I'd imagined when I first planned to move there, we rode back to Ramallah. I was dropped off at my house and they continued to theirs—a bittersweet ending to a lovely day.

✦ ✦ ✦

I started reading. *Faith and Freedom—Women's Human Rights in the Muslim World,* edited by Mahnaz Afkhami. I was drawn to a chapter entitled "They Insult Us and We Elect Them," contributed by Toujan al-Faisal, the first (and only) elected female member of the Jordanian parliament. Divorced with three children, she had spoken out against issues such as polygamy, wife beating, and corruption. She had publicly challenged Islamic fundamentalists over their laws and called the king's power into question.

As a result, she was charged with apostasy—opposing Islam—by the Islamic court. The punishment: execution. Her trial, which spanned 1989–1990, had attracted international attention, and her courage had surpassed the expectations of even her most loyal followers. The final verdict was still undecided when I decided to get in touch with her in the spring of 2000.

I tracked down her phone number through friends in Jordan and called her, explaining that I was living in the Middle East and speaking to women who had challenged laws or conditions they considered unfair. To my delight, she was eager to speak about her work. I arranged to travel to Jordan to see her, taking the customary trip through Jericho and crossing the Jordan River.

Jordan was pleasant and calm on the surface. There were no checkpoints or gun-toting civilians as in Palestine. I arrived at Toujan's apartment in Amman in the late afternoon. Knocking on her door, I envisioned a woman warrior, an Amazon. The door opened and, for a moment, I was speechless. Before me stood a petite, fragile-looking middle-aged woman with long brown hair, sporting a stylish sundress and heels. She let me in and began chatting right away.

"Welcome to the 'Kingdom!'" she laughed as I followed her inside. "Jordan uses the word *kingdom* so it can project the image of a fairy tale. I fight for democracy, but our true form of government is fear—fear of punishment in both the mortal and the immortal world."

The atmosphere clashed with her fiery rhetoric. The home was perfectly serene, with her three teenage daughters sitting at a dining room table, quietly doing their homework. She introduced us, and right away I knew that I wasn't in the company of a typical Arab family: I could tell she was head of the household, confident and strong without a man. She continued to talk to me while her children were within earshot, her daughters occasionally looking up from their studies to give a nod of support.

The contrast between her and Dina was enormous. Dina so shy and humble, needed constant reassurance that whatever she said was accurate. Toujan, in contrast, had chosen public life; she wasn't born into it. She answered my questions almost before I asked them.

In the early 1970s, when she was in her twenties, she was offered a job at Jordan's only television station, which was owned by the government. "I think I was hired because they liked my looks," she said. "I wasn't concerned about politics at the time, but I decided to take the camera into the streets and use it like a pen, to tell stories. And I discovered there was a lot of suffering. I decided to look at our taboos."

In the beginning, the government trusted her. Her TV programs examined poverty, discrimination, and women's rights. But once she began to explore the sources of economic suffering, which she believed was caused by government corruption, fraud, bribery, and even the counterfeiting of currency, strange things began to happen: her files started mysteriously disappearing, and she began to receive anonymous threats. Instead of backing down, she became an advocate of political reform. She publicly demanded answers and asked for elections, democracy, transparency. Much to the government's chagrin, there was little they could do. Dismissing her might have caused an uproar from the community.

During this time, Toujan was pregnant with her second child. The pressure and the anonymous warnings continued unabated, and she found the stress physically exhausting. Her baby was born prematurely and died several hours later. Once this happened, she said, "I felt my baby has given its life for this conflict. It made me militant. I thought, it's going to be worth it. I never felt fear after that. No one could make me pay a higher price."

In 1988, the country was gearing up to hold its first parliamentary elections since 1967, when Israel won its war with Jordan. Toujan had been involved in proposing new laws. Then she realized that if she wanted these laws to be presented and passed, she'd better run herself.

Her platform was built on two pillars: democracy and transparency. During her campaign, she accused King Hussein of tampering with the constitution. According to Toujan, he gave himself the right to dissolve parliament if he saw fit. She claimed that this was an unconstitutional amendment, and she wrote about it. The king was furious. Until these elections, the Muslim Brotherhood had been the only group allowed to share any power with the king, who allowed Islamic law to be incorporated into his kingdom. The king publicly rejected Toujan's allegations and reminded the fundamentalists that it was he who allowed them to have a voice when no other party was permitted. She was up against the fundamentalists *and* the state.

"The Brotherhood got the message to go after me," she said. "They said to the king, 'We will protect you, and we will stand beside you during these allegations.' They don't like that democracy allows you to challenge sharia and Islamic law. I was always challenging and proving that their interpretation of Islam was wrong. I wanted to give the power to the people. Democracy means man can't rule in the name of God, and the king no longer has all the power. So the king and the [Brotherhood] joined hands, and they [called for] a death sentence."

"Just like that?" I asked.

"The Brotherhood accused me of being against Islam, and they called for a trial," she said. "The punishment for apostasy is execution. It was a case built out of nothing."

Toujan's outspokenness not only drew the attention of groups such as the Muslim Brotherhood; it also had alarming repercussions for her family. Toujan told me about an incident in which her relatives had been victims of violence at a social gathering. She'd been sitting in a large banquet room at a table with her husband and other family members. Suddenly the room went dark, and tablecloths were thrown over her head as well as her husband's. Blinded, they were thrown into a closet and couldn't get out. It was only after an hour that they learned it was their own supporters who had thrown them there for protection. They emerged to find that many of their family members had sustained serious injuries. With the country watching and her trial date rapidly approaching, Toujan decided not to show up in court.

But she soon changed her position and decided to stand up to the fundamentalists. They tried to make her husband divorce her since, in Islam, an apostate cannot be married. He refused. (They did divorce a decade later, but on their own terms.) Jordanians rallied around her. The king, surprised by the extent of her support, had to appear distanced and impartial. Watching this showdown, he finally stepped in and asked that her trial be indefinitely postponed.

She lost the election, but that did not stop her from delving into the dark corners of her government and continuing to challenge the fundamentalists. Toujan secured her position as the voice of the people. She continued to make TV programs that challenged oppressive laws. All the while, I had been trying to navigate the laws that granted Marwan complete control over my children and, indirectly, over me. I asked Toujan why the Koran dictated that children should be taken from their mother in the case of divorce. She explained that the Prophet Muhammad said that children should leave the mother when they were about thirteen, because when the Koran was written, this was the age that children were considered grown and ready for marriage. The intention was not to separate a mother from a growing child. Fundamentalists hadn't modernized their interpretation, instead holding on to this archaic rule to instill fear of divorce. Toujan assured me that Islam didn't condemn me, only a bitter group of men interpreting it. In general, she felt these laws were designed to do one thing above all else: keep women hidden and silent.

Despite the risks, Toujan decided to run again in the 1993 elections. This time she won, making her the first elected female member of parliament. When the results were in, the king appointed two more women as members, which Toujan believes was a hollow gesture to appear progressive. Toujan's victory seemed to be an indicator that the country was ready for women to be part of the political process, but the other women weren't qualified, she said, and that weakened the female position in general. However, Toujan's position made it difficult for the king to throw her in jail when she challenged the government. "The whole Arab world was watching to see how the king would handle my actions," she said.

Toujan used her new position to tackle the laws of sharia. I discovered when investigating the laws pertaining to the custody of my children that Islamic law is derived from several sources. Some laws are "revealed" as a divine code. These are permanent, nonnegotiable laws. Some laws are based on "unrevealed" messages and are open to interpretation. Many of the Islamic laws

covering personal status, such as marriage, divorce, and child custody, vary among sects of Islam and from country to country, but
there is one common thread: men are able to control women
through these laws. Toujan tried to teach women through her TV
show that these laws were misinterpreted, that Islam was never
intended to suppress women.

A movement was beginning to sweep Jordan. Toujan had followed the movement—its growth, actions, positions, writings,
and recruitment of women. "They are afraid God will punish
them if they don't agree. Women who are 'enlightened' start by
breaking the other women up into categories within the group, a
structure made of 'mothers,' 'daughters,' 'sisters' and so on,
depending on their knowledge of Islam. It's a man-made concept.
In Islam, no such hierarchy exists. These women have an initiation ceremony for the newcomers. They seat the newcomers at a
table, and the enlightened women encircle the new recruits and
sing. A womblike atmosphere is created, encompassing the
woman, making her feel everything is safe as long as she is one of
them."

Toujan occasionally confronted the fundamentalists, judges,
and enforcers of the sharia publicly. She once challenged on TV a
head sheik who had previously appeared on a program instruct-
ing men how to beat their wives. The religious sheik had declared
that it was "God's given right," because women needed to be dis-
ciplined. Beating a wife was necessary for her own good. If she
behaved improperly, she could be thrown out on the streets by an
unhappy husband, shamed by society.

"They also instructed men not to beat their wives over the
head, because this is where the beauty is," she said. "Women are
like merchandise."

On air, the cleric told her that a husband should beat his wife,
as if he were the boss.

"Do you tell men who are bosses to beat their employees?" she asked him. "Where in the Koran does it say that you can beat your wife?"

Unable to justify his statements, he finally retracted them.

In another incident, Toujan attended a lecture given by a female fundamentalist. She challenged the content of a handbook distributed to women about "how to be obedient and how to serve" their husbands. Then the lecturer read a verse from the Koran, and the women started chanting, repeating the prayers with music. The woman was trying to dissuade women from voting, saying that this should be left up to their husbands. When Toujan started to argue, they protested: "No questions, no arguments allowed!"

"Western women have more economic independence and the social pressures are less. Arab women are blamed for bad marriages or no children. Nothing is the man's fault. If a Western woman is battered, she can do things. Arab women are told not to shame the family. But there is more exploitation of women, commercially, in the West. Here, no one would harass a woman at her job. Divorced women in the West can marry someone more appropriate and of higher status than their first husband. A divorced woman in the Middle East has to move home and return her children to the husband. The family watches her very closely because she's no longer a virgin, and they think she may be tempted. Then they try to marry her off to prove she's still good. She's usually forced to marry someone of lower status."

Toujan's former husband was a doctor whom she left because she wanted complete freedom. Perhaps she knew this from the outset: conventional sharia doesn't allow women to divorce men, so she had drawn up a premarital agreement that stipulated that she could divorce him if she so chose. Because she exercised the option, people called her a shrew. Her husband, meanwhile, sent an article to the newspapers praising his wife.

Few men were similarly enlightened. I told her about the girls I'd met who were trying to protect themselves from honor killings. Toujan had found that most honor killings were committed because of incest, usually with a younger brother. If the girl is proved not to be a virgin, the court condones the killings. Toujan confronted a religious sheik about the religious support of this, and he finally admitted it wasn't in the Koran; in fact, the Koran forbids the honor killing of women. When Western journalists had come to her home a few years earlier and she told them about honor killings, they went back home and wrote about it.

"It became embarrassing to Jordan, so they decided to do something about it," she said.

It took the Western world to get the fundamentalists to change their ways, much to Toujan's chagrin. The maximum sentence for an honor killing now is four to five years, and release is possible after one year.

"The only way to change our laws is through attention from outsiders," she said. "Now that they know outsiders are watching, Jordan wants to appear progressive and now people will dig out the dirt. That's why I wanted to meet with you, so you could be our messenger."

Soon enough it was time for me to head home. She left me with these words: "Everyone has the power to change the future. Especially the women. Most women have never learned they can stand up to someone who abuses them. It would help if they would at least raise their children to know that they can stand up for themselves. Children *must* learn to stand up for themselves, and wives must stand up to their husbands, their families, their states."

On my way back to the border, I thought how interesting it was that the women I met in the Middle East seemed to have their own brand of feminism. They wanted Western rights, but they also loved their femininity. They didn't feel that they had to choose between their family and a career. There was no stigma attached to staying home and being a housewife. To me, it seemed these women thought the two weren't mutually exclusive. They valued their lives inside and outside the home.

I thought back to Mai Yamani, a woman I had met in London years ago. Our mutual friend Nabila Khashoggi had made the introduction by phone, and we arranged to meet at her home and then go out for dinner. Mai was from Saudi Arabia and had a doctorate in anthropology from Oxford; she was also the daughter of one of the most powerful men in the world, Sheik Yamani, who had been Saudi Arabia's oil minister between 1962 and 1986 and the leader of OPEC. Mai had edited a book, *Islam and Feminism: Legal and Literary Perspectives.* I went to her five-story home in London early in the evening. As soon as I walked in, she told me she had a feeling we were old friends, although we had just met. She led me into one of the many beautifully decorated reception rooms.

"Would you like to sit on Cleopatra's chair?" she asked, pointing to a carved Egyptian antique. She told me she collected ancient Egyptian costumes and usually put them on before sitting there.

At the time of our meeting, she was in charge of the Royal Institute for International Affairs. Much of her work was focused on the political, religious, and cultural mind-set of Saudi Arabia and other Arab countries—specifically, the sharia.

"The image of Arabs can change, and we can still remain Arab," she explained. "The image doesn't have to be Western. Although I have learned a lot from the West, I must have my own identity."

Mai refused to be considered the least bit Western simply because she wasn't Western.

"Arab men have a tendency to put you in this category if you are professional, if you have a job," she said.

The day before, Mai had had two TV interviews, and she wore a short skirt. From time to time Mai would say, "*Bis me la*," which means, "In the name of Allah." The female interviewer ogled Mai's skirt and finally demanded: "How can you say 'In the name of Allah' and wear that short skirt!"

"I don't think God cares what I wear," she told her. "I have my relationship with God whether I wear a long skirt or a short one."

Not long after my meeting with Toujan, I attended a meeting of the Women's Technical Committee, an activist group of Palestinians who were accompanied by women from the U.N. Development Program. They were coming together in an effort to ask Hamas women to sign a petition requesting that religious laws be transferred to the civil courts. The meeting was held in a large hall and attended by 400 Hamas women. At the front of the hall was our host: a sheik, unconventionally dressed in a leather coat and jeans.

The woman from the technical committee presented their petition. The sheik then read his own petition: "We demand that personal status laws stay in the domain of the Islamic courts." The sheik began to yell, "Who agrees with my statement? Sign if you do. Whoever agrees raise your hand. [With this, his followers raised their hands.] As always, let us express ourselves. This is your personal view. Now, we'll let this woman speak." His words sounded fair, but his tone of voice and penetrating gaze were frightening.

Taking her turn, the Women's Technical Committee representative stepped up and said, "You are all intelligent and can read, so it's my moral and religious duty to give you exact information. Religion is for peace for all times and places, religion is for sympathy and love. Religion is never about violence, hate, and discrimination. In the conference on violence, Sheik Toufik, a scholar in Islamic thought, agrees with us and approves of our principles. Our views stem from the sharia; they are Islamic in words and in spirit."

The sheik railed on in response: "Who supports violence? Did I say I want violence? These women are making problems. They focus attention on problems. They say, 'Look, here is a woman in Jericho who is being abused by her husband. Poor woman! Everyone look! Take a photo!' Do you really think that men will stand by and passively watch as women are trying to change these laws to control them?"

The women were mesmerized, hundreds of eyes watching him as he whipped himself into a rage, pacing back and forth.

He continued, "The women's technical committee has published a book called *Law and the Future of the Palestinian Women*. This book was funded by the United Nations Development Program. Now the UNDP is going to teach us about Islam? And about human rights? As you see, the West is not very concerned with such issues, especially in our countries. They just want to disrupt family life so they can dominate us. Do not sign this petition! Do you think these people who write books about human rights know more about our laws than we do here? They know more about our religion than we do here?"

A woman from the technical committee stepped up. "No, we are a country that asks for democracy."

"Yes, American democracy!"

"No one is adopting Western slogans! If you hear any of us using these slogans, you can criticize us. We are talking about human rights before we are talking about laws. You know we have cases of girls raped by their fathers. Where are the laws that are going to protect them?"

The sheik interrupted: "The women in this gathering, out of

respect for our Islamic faith, are rejecting the Westernizing of our Palestinian women. After listening to suggestions, we demand that the Islamic courts and Islamic judges are the only authority that can suggest changes in the personal status laws."

"Our laws should be under public discussion. Many of these laws made in the name of Islam are actually against what Islam says," the committee woman insisted.

"If they think we are going to enter a dialogue with them they are mistaken, because they are the devil!" the sheik yelled.

With that, the Hamas women began to chant like the chorus of a Greek tragedy: "God is great, God is great!"

This was what Toujan had spoken of. *This* was rule by fear.

CHAPTER THIRTEEN

Going Home

I RETURNED FROM SEEING TOUJAN IN EARLY MAY 2000. Rain hadn't yet come to the West Bank, which remained dry and barren. The atmosphere mirrored the mood of the people. I sensed tension starting to build with the oncoming summer heat. The new roads and housing, water supplies, phones, agriculture, job opportunities, new hospitals, and access to medical care that were supposed to have taken place as a result of the peace signing were slow to come. Some blamed corruption in the Palestinian government; others blamed a lack of money from the donor countries that had committed to building Palestine. Many of the ministers were building villas and driving expensive cars, while people in camps struggled to survive. People told me stories of Mafia-type leaders who threatened small business owners if they did not hand over a percentage of their earnings.

One day I had spent several hours in an Internet café located in the back of a building on Ramallah's main street. When I walked out, I was amazed to see hundreds of people on the streets chanting in Arabic and holding signs. I had to work my way through the dense crowd of men, who were yelling about their frustrations at the government and corruption. I wove through the pack, only to be faced by another pack, this one of women. It was a segregated uprising. Nonetheless, it was exhilarating to feel that energy in the streets.

Those streets were now still. Tractors sat unattended; building and infrastructure projects were left abandoned. New restaurants, once filled, were empty. Money was tight, and government employees were going long periods without pay. The pace at which hope could disappear from people's lives was frightening.

I loved to walk through the Old City and see the sights, and so it wasn't unusual that I happened to take a trip into Jerusalem on May 14, unaware that it was the fifty-second anniversary of the founding of Israel. An Israeli parade marched through the Arab side of Jerusalem, with participants carrying signs declaring Jerusalem their capital. The claim to Jerusalem was still an unresolved issue of the DOP. I was on the east side, the Arab side, observing the reactions of those who felt that this was the anniversary of the loss of their homeland. Simmering hostilities exploded, and fighting broke out in the streets. Suddenly Israeli police and army tanks were storming in, and five Palestinians were killed in the violence.

A new round of peace talks was scheduled to take place during the summer. According to the time line under the Declaration of Principles, the final-status regulations had to be completed by September 13, 2000. President Clinton invited

Prime Minister Ehud Barak and Yasir Arafat for a summit at Camp David, Maryland, on July 11. The meeting would deal with the most difficult issues: the right of return, compensation for Palestinian refugees from 1948 and from the 1967 war, and the final status of Jerusalem—who would rule it, or would it be divided? The issues of Israeli settlements, security arrangements, and boundaries would also be on the agenda.

Thanks to Marwan's high position in the government, Deena and Tarik were largely sheltered from the cruel realities of life in the Middle East during this period. My children were busy with end-of-the-year activities at school. They had become attached to their friends, teachers, and the school community. They were socially active but also well chaperoned. Independence to them was having their guard wait in the car instead of accompanying them inside when visiting friends. Despite these precautions, one day while riding to school in their chauffeured car, Deena and Tarik saw a Palestinian dragged from his vehicle and beaten by Israeli soldiers. They had no idea what had provoked the beating.

When Riyad, their driver, dropped them off, he came to see me at work and told me what happened and that the children were extremely upset. He warned me that there would probably be even more unrest at the border in the days and weeks to come. With Marwan traveling, Riyad was especially concerned about their return trip home that afternoon.

"I'm going to go with you to pick them up," I said. He wasn't keen on the idea, but I was insistent. He took his role of protector very seriously.

Several hours later, as we sat in line at the border, Riyad became alarmed. He drew my attention to a group of young children standing on the roof of a building, throwing rocks at armed Israeli soldiers stationed at the checkpoint below. They were a ragged bunch: skinny legs, dusty shorts and T-shirts. Suddenly I heard gunfire, and it seemed to be directed at the roof where the children were standing. Dirt flew everywhere, and the children scrambled down an outdoor staircase. They must have noticed that our car had government tags and therefore couldn't be shot at, because they ran toward us.

"Get down!" Riyad shouted. I looked in the other direction and saw eight soldiers in gas masks toting huge guns, which I later learned were tear-gas guns, charging toward our car. Riyad tried to maneuver the car out of danger, while I yelled for him not to expose the crouching children.

Riyad had ten children himself, and he'd been caught in other cross-fires. I hadn't, and it haunted me for nights. My children became afraid to go to school, and I couldn't bear the sight of machine guns.

Fortunately, the school year was drawing to a close. I agreed to go to an amusement park in Israel with the children as part of an end-of-the-year school trip, volunteering with several other parents to chaperone. The park was full of Israeli settlers wearing civilian clothing and rifles slung like backpacks over their shoulders. I complained to the amusement park's manager, explaining that this was a place for children to escape from the horrors of war.

"You shouldn't be concerned," the manager told me. "People check their bullets at the door."

Incidents like this made me even more homesick. I missed my culture. I missed my rights. I was proud that although I didn't have custody of the children, they'd watched me respond to the situation proactively instead of sitting idly by. They knew I'd fought for them and that I had spent several years in a difficult environment because being close to them was my top priority. My ex-husband was powerful because of his position, but I wanted to show them a different kind of power. They knew the stories of the women I'd met. I shared my experiences with them every chance

I could. My struggle mirrored those of all the women around me. My desire for resolution with Marwan was minor compared with the outreach I'd seen taking place between Palestinians and Israelis. My children seemed happy, and I was satisfied knowing that I'd not infused their lives with any of my personal distress.

My daughter wrote an essay for school on the meaning of work. She wrote it about me. She wrote that she knew her mother had given up many things in the United States to be with her and her brother, but she also saw that my work in the Middle East was effective. She learned from watching me that accomplishing something requires working hard and refusing to let anything get in the way. It was a simplistic observation maybe, but it touched me deeply. I knew my fifteen-year-old daughter understood.

Meanwhile, Marwan was preoccupied with the upcoming peace talks. I told the children that I needed to take a trip to the States that summer. I continued to struggle financially, and political tensions were mounting, so my job could be on the line. I wanted to see if there was any work I could arrange to do in the Middle East for Western news stations. In addition, the minister of broadcasting was keen on my traveling back to the United States. He wanted me to pursue Arabic-language episodes of *Sesame Street*, speak with satellite companies to increase programming selections in the West Bank, and solicit funds for conflict resolution projects between Palestinians and Israelis in the media. After that, I'd return to the Middle East.

I'd barely saved enough money to buy a ticket. The children began asking Marwan if they could visit the States too. It had been over three years since the children had been back, and they wanted to see their extended family. At first he refused, but the children pushed him. By then, Tarik was thirteen years old and Deena was fifteen. Both children had formed close friendships and bonds in the Middle East. Marwan had succeeded in excluding me from the lay decisions affecting my children's lives; he had created their world on his terms, in his home. In a sense he had won. He took from me the most important thing: a home with my children. Now I looked at my children, grown up into teenagers, nearly independent. It was too late. I couldn't replace those years, and I couldn't pull them away from everything they had learned to love, everything he had offered them while belittling my role. Even if he allowed them to travel to the States, he and I both knew that it would be impossible for us to resume our previous lives there. Even if I could financially provide for us in the States, he had already conditioned them socially and emotionally. If I kept them in the States, they would miss their friends. He knew that.

And so he finally consented to their pleas for a visit. He bought them round-trip tickets, and we arranged to fly on the same plane. Riyad and Marwan took us to the airport in Tel Aviv. Known for their scrupulous security checks and in-depth questioning at the airport, we were spared this due to Marwan's VIP government privileges. He allowed me to be part of his "family" so that I would not be subject to the searches. Marwan suggested to the children that he would arrange to meet them for a shopping trip in Europe on their way back.

I wanted to do what was best for the children. I would win this battle by remembering that my goal was to be a messenger for the women I had met. I wouldn't dwell on my personal experience, but instead I could remember it was the experience of many women. If I insisted the children stay in the States, I would be imposing financial and emotional hardship, and I couldn't subject my children to this. I would have to continue being their mother from a distance, making my visits to their home and being treated like an outsider. My alternatives were grim. At least I knew if we returned, I could see them, and they would continue to live comfortably.

The children and I were excited about seeing the rest of our family and enjoying simple pleasures like wide-screen movies, shopping centers, and favorite foods. I felt grateful for the laws in our country, especially for women, even if they weren't always enforced. At least we had them; someone had fought for them, and we could press for these rights to be respected. My mother and stepfather met us at the airport in Washington, D.C., where they'd relocated. It was nice to sink into a comfortable bed, my children and I back as though nothing had changed.

But everything had changed. My father had just been released from prison. I'd had very little contact with him, only messages through my brothers. The judge who oversaw his trial had passed away. In a new ruling, his sentence was shortened before his appeal was heard, and they released him after three years instead of five. He wasn't allowed to leave California yet, part of the restrictions that went with his release. When he spoke, he seemed different, calmer, more humble, but he was anxious to start a new company and build another empire. He was determined to "save the family." We were all fine and didn't want any "saving"; we just wanted him to focus on his own life. My brothers were doing very well and built successful lives on their own, and I was pursuing my own opportunities too. I knew my father's life was going to be difficult. He could not practice law again and had no capital to start a business. But thoughts of "saving the family" gave him a purpose.

My brothers helped him move into a small apartment in Newport, California, where we hoped he would enjoy his days relaxing by the pool. He said he was going to take some time to think about what he wanted to do in the future. My brothers went to visit him after they had furnished his apartment and discovered that he had gotten rid of all the furniture and replaced it with desks and computers, lining them up in his living and dining room. He was preparing to run an office again, and he was ready to fill the empty chairs.

My children and I spent a pleasant summer together, staying with my brothers, mother, and stepfather. The children were happy swimming, shopping, taking trips into Washington, and playing with their cousins. Some of their schoolmates from Jerusalem were also visiting family in the States, so they were able to visit with them as well. It seemed as if they had never left. I savored my time with them, with no one coming between us, no one watching us.

Meanwhile, peace talks were taking place at Camp David while Marwan remained in Gaza with his constituents. No press was allowed inside Camp David. The leaders of the peace talks had thought they would make more progress if the press wasn't reporting and their citizens weren't reacting until they finished. Regardless, Arafat had chosen one journalist to accompany him— a woman who had been a close friend and neighbor of mine in Ramallah. I spent several days with her in Frederick, Maryland, while the talks were going on. At night she would secretly meet Arafat's guards on a darkened road, and they would hand over notes he specifically sent for her regarding the progress of the talks. She would then leak his messages to the media, in the hopes that the news would reach his people and provide reassurance.

The talks lasted fourteen days, but nothing was resolved. They couldn't reach agreements on the key issues, such as the right of refugees to return or the control of Jerusalem. Both sides blamed the other for the failure, for wanting too much. And both sides had many factions back home that would not have accepted compromises. Before leaving, Arafat, Israeli Prime Minister Barak, and President Clinton signed an agreement to continue negotiations for a just and lasting peace. Marwan and I never discussed this turn of events.

✦ ✦ ✦

I felt sad as our summer was coming to an end, and the children were ready to return to Ramallah for school. I still hadn't finished pursuing some projects for my work and would stay behind.

I took them to the airport. They were sad to go, but like most other teenagers, they were excited to reconnect with their friends. I reassured them I would follow shortly. After they left, I sat in the airport for an hour or so, overwhelmed by a feeling of deep emptiness.

I spoke to Deena and Tarik several times after their arrival. They didn't mention anything unusual, but nightly news reports announced the failure of the peace talks and the deteriorating hopes of peace between Palestine and Israel. The hope that had carried these people through the past seven years was dwindling fast. I watched news reports of increasing violence. When I asked the children about them, they insisted it looked a lot worse on TV, just as I had responded when I was there. They said they were perfectly safe. Marwan's wife had come to visit them from her other home in Tunisia and was helping to watch them while Marwan worked. I wasn't sure if she had decided to make more of an effort to be in the West Bank because she wanted to make sure I wasn't going to spend so much time at Marwan's house when I returned or if Marwan had asked her, figuring they would have an easier time to be together since my presence had upset her. Her children from her first marriage, about the same ages as my children, had come with her.

On the morning of September 28, 2000, Marwan told the children that he didn't want them going to school. "Trust me," he told them. "There will be problems today."

That afternoon, former Israeli defense minister Ariel Sharon decided to visit the Temple Mount in Jerusalem to demonstrate the rights of the Jews. Sovereignty over this site was a major source of contention, and many Palestinians interpreted this move as a provocation. Sovereignty over the holy mount had been a major stumbling block in the peace process. The site hosts Judaism's most sacred shrine, the Western Wall, and is home to two major mosques and the Dome of the Rock.

From that day on, more and more Palestinians took to the streets in protest. Deena and Tarik told me they heard gunfire day and night. They tried to visit a friend one day, and their car was caught in more cross fire. They called to tell me what happened and that they had arrived safely, but then the phone line was cut. I sat in front of the television, crying, watching the footage of tanks rolling down familiar streets in Ramallah, streets that now looked like a war zone. Many Israelis claimed that Arafat supported and encouraged the uprising against occupation, while Arafat and his government claimed they were unable to control it.

Whenever the phone rang, I grabbed it, hoping it was the children. Finally, after several days of calling everyone I had met in the Middle East who had a phone and not getting one call through, I heard from Marwan. He'd taken the children to Jordan. When I asked for more information, he put the children on. It broke my heart to hear them so distressed so far away. They told me they had had time to grab only a few items from their rooms before tanks were going to block them in. They were accustomed to gunfire, but this was worse than ever before.

Deena threw some clothes in a bag; Tarik took a basketball. As they fled to Jordan, the only other vehicles on the road were tanks. They were shaken and confused, but now safe at a hotel with Marwan and his wife. I begged Marwan to send them back to me. He screamed at me that he wasn't sending them anywhere and told me not to call. I believed he was still in denial that a war was breaking out. He still wanted to believe the peace process was working. Admitting the danger would be like giving up. He insisted nothing was wrong, that everything would settle down in a few days, and that he was taking them back to Ramallah, "where they belonged."

For over a week, I had no contact with them. I was frantic. The West Bank had erupted into a battleground. I phoned Marwan daily, but he wouldn't take my calls. I asked Palestinian ambassador Hassan Abdul Rahman in Washington to speak with him, but to no avail. I was frantic. Each time I saw a burning building on the news, I feared Marwan had taken the children back to Ramallah.

Then I received a call from Marwan's wife. She told me that Marwan had returned to Palestine to be with Arafat. He'd wanted to take the children, but checked with authorities and was told that he wouldn't be allowed to bring them through the border. He was, however, planning to return for them. She allowed them to call me, for which I remain extremely grateful. Deena and Tarik still seemed confused, telling me that Marwan insisted everything would be fine in a few days, that *he* could decide what was safe. It broke my heart to hang up, leaving my children crying half a world away.

Violence was now rampant in Gaza and Ramallah, and he was still planning to bring them back there. What little connection I had with them was through his wife, who was sympathetic and understood, as a parent, that I was desperate to have my children with me. I begged her to put the children on a plane to me before he returned, but she hesitated. She told me she was already defying Marwan by letting the children speak to me. To send them would be an enormous betrayal. Besides, she said, Marwan had taken them into Jordan without U.S. passports, making it virtually impossible for them to get back into the States.

I decided to take matters into my own hands in order to bring my children back home. I called my cousin Donna Shalala, who was still in President Clinton's cabinet. Maybe she could help me through the State Department. All the while, I was terrified Marwan would return for them before I could make arrangements. Calling Donna's office, I was told she was away for several days.

I called Marwan's wife back an hour or so later. She nervously told me that the American embassy in Jordan had just shut down and that the last plane for America was leaving the following afternoon. As an American herself, she was uncomfortable there, sensing a strong hostility against Americans by fundamentalists. She wanted to leave for her home in Tunis and was willing to send my children to me if I could get the passports. She had some contacts at the embassy and would try on her end as well. I called Donna's office again and asked to speak to one of her directors in international relations, someone I had met through Donna several times. He understood the urgency of the situation and told me he would locate Donna right away.

I sat by the phone, unable to move, helpless to do anything but wait for it to ring again. I watched the hands creeping forward on the clock and imagined with each minute that Marwan was one step closer to Amman, where he would take my children away with him into a war zone. After the longest three hours of my life, the director called me back. He had spoken to Donna. Given the exigent circumstances, they would call the American ambassador in Jordan, although it was 3:00 A.M. there, and ask for new passports to be issued and for arrangements to be made for my children to be on the plane. They said they would call me back when they had any information.

I felt as if I had walked from Ramallah to Amman and back by the time the phone rang early in the morning at my brother's house in Maryland. Donna's office informed me that when they reached the ambassador, he had already been informed of the situation by attachés who knew Marwan's wife. The ambassador was already in the process of issuing the passports. They assured me that the passports would be ready and that my children would be on the plane.

I spoke again with Marwan's wife. She wanted to avoid speaking with Marwan before she put them on the plane so she could tell him after the fact. This also meant that she had no idea where he was—he could be on his way back. We were focusing on getting the paperwork finished and making it on time to the airport.

Finally, I heard the words I had waited to hear for weeks: the children were on the plane, on their way to the States, and she would have to break the news to Marwan.

◆

I sat alone at Dulles Airport in Virginia, staring at the electronic Arrivals board displaying my children's flight information. For the first time in weeks, I allowed myself to take a deep breath. I paced the hallways, exhausted yet exhilarated at the thought of Deena and Tarik coming home. I looked out the windows at the chilly October night sky, the lights flickering from incoming planes and distant stars. I remembered how excited I used to get as a child when I spotted a plane flying through the night. I always wondered what exotic place it was coming from and what stories and memories its passengers were carrying with them. Now I had my own story: the cowed woman who boarded the plane to the Middle East several years ago was not the same woman who had returned.

I looked again at the Arrivals board. The flight had landed! The tension and anxiety of the past three years seemed to melt from my body in a single moment. I wasn't sure what I thought would happen when I saw my children, but I expected them to be as relieved as I was, happy to be safe. But when I greeted them at the gate, they looked tired and distracted, as though they had brought the war home with them. They just wanted to go back to my mother's house and sleep. They asked questions about their father—if he was safe, if he knew they were on their way, if he was angry, how long they were staying, where they were going to live and go to school.

We went to my mother's home in Maryland and called Marwan. He was short with me, having by now been told by his wife that the children were on their way to the States. When I put them on the phone, he told them that they would be with me for only a short time.

I let them sleep and offered them American things they loved, like their favorite candies and videos, trying to make them comfortable. I called Marwan's wife to thank her. She said that Marwan had seemed angry but admitted it would probably be some time before he would be able to leave. There was a war going on, and he couldn't leave Arafat or his country.

I watched CNN the next day and saw more escalation and frustrated people with no solutions. The children sat next to me and watched the footage in disbelief. Marwan appeared on the news frequently as Arafat's spokesman. Suddenly a life they had been living and a father they had lived with were realities they could experience only by watching headline news. They seemed agitated by the news reports, which they perceived as inaccurate and imbalanced, not showing the true picture of the Palestinian people.

I let them ease into the new environment. My daughter spent several nights crying. I was convinced they were suffering from a bit of posttraumatic stress. They were both sensitive, quiet, and withdrawn. I let them take the lead.

With the 2000 U.S. presidential elections several weeks away, the future of Middle East policies was uncertain. I hoped to offer the children some stability and let them settle in. I wanted to enroll them in school. Meanwhile, Marwan called them every day, insisting that things would get better and that he would be bringing them back. We continued seeing him on TV in the Gaza Strip, speaking on Arafat's behalf. He always looked elegant, perfectly dressed and groomed, while bullets flew in the background. I wondered how he managed to maintain such an impeccable appearance in the midst of war.

The phone calls that went back and forth for the next three weeks were always the same: I wanted him to stop telling the children they were returning, and I wanted moral and financial support to establish a secure home environment in the States for them; he refused, still hoping that the political situation would change. But eventually he conceded the situation did not look as if it would improve in the near future. Because of his political obligations and the dangers in the area, it would be best to keep the children in the United States. He agreed to pay child support and get the children set up in a new home with me.

Tarik and Deena were still withdrawn, but at least they knew they'd be staying. Now I could enroll them in school. We took a town house outside Washington, near my two brothers and their children. I accepted a position as executive director of Women in Film, a large nonprofit organization, and we began our new lives together. By then it was the middle of October. Deena was going into the tenth grade and Tarik into the eighth. They hated having to go to a big public school. Their school in Ramallah, after all, had just fifty students. It was a difficult adjustment for them: they missed their father, their friends, and their home. My daughter continued to spend her nights crying and once asked that I take her to a hospital because she couldn't stop sobbing and she couldn't understand why. I held her instead.

Slowly they adjusted. The support of my mother and stepfather, my brothers, their wives, and their children was critical, and it became the core of the children's strength. Each wrote separately the following year in a school assignment what this experience was like.

My son wrote: "When the uprising started, I was 13. My life and the lives of those around me was about to change for the worse. Staying in Jordan during the uprising, all I could do was pray, but the problems seemed to escalate. When I learned I was going back to America the news hit me hard. My sister didn't handle it well either, but we found ourselves looking to each other for comfort. The thought of leaving my dad and friends was emotionally draining. Starting my new life in Maryland was difficult. The school was over ten times larger than the one I left and I couldn't focus while I watched the death toll increasing in Palestine. Overcoming and adjusting to a new life is not easy, but I learned to accept the present and fondly remember the past."

Deena wrote: "One day in October 2000, my brother and I were evacuated and sent back to America without our father. The evacuation process was the most difficult time in my life, and my brother and I depended on each other and became each other's pillars. Living back in the U.S. was hard. I was confused and lacked goals other than to get back to Ramallah. My mother was a strong instrument in helping me adjust. She forced me to participate in activities such as dance classes, soccer, babysitting and tutoring my four cousins. My life finally began to take shape and I became a happy teenager."

Over time, our home became filled with the new friends they made. They seemed to get more and more used to their new life. Their close friends, ones who used to stay over with them at Marwan's house, moved back to the States as well and stayed with us briefly. This was very therapeutic for the children, as I know it was difficult explaining their background to many of their new friends. My work was fulfilling. Again, I was working with a group of women who were trying to improve the lives of other women, this time in the entertainment industry. My organization was supportive in allowing me to reach out to Palestinian and Israeli screenwriters who were willing to work together on reconciliation. The political atmosphere in the Middle East continued to decline, however. We watched Marwan on nightly talk shows, and the children were proud of his work. He phoned them daily. We finally got along as two parents who were concerned only about their children. What was between us personally began to seem unimportant. I had my children back with me in the States, and finally, my home and theirs was the same.

EPILOGUE

DESPITE THE COUNTLESS HEADLINES ABOUT THE MIDDLE East, tales of oppression and destruction, the opulence of royalty and the ravages of war, there are many more stories that do not get told, especially those of the peacemakers.

Robi Damelin's efforts continue through the Parents Circle. They continue to reach out to other parents who have lost children, both Palestinian and Israeli. Their efforts were involved in placing a phone line that runs between the Gaza Strip and Israel. This phone number functions like a hot line. Families, some Palestinian, some Israeli, are able to speak across "enemy" lines to share their grief. They help each other heal the shared pain that connects them despite existing barriers. In the first two years after its inception, 800,000 hours of phone calls were placed.

The governments have failed, but people are taking peace into their own hands. An eye-opening film called *Encounter Point*, made by Israeli filmmaker Ronit Avri, shows the diplomacy taking place between citizens. Not unlike the American civil rights movement or other movements of change, it came from the people. Ronit Avri's organization, Just Vision, has compiled a list of 160 organizations formed by Palestinians and Israelis over the last few years in an effort to bring peace. These are the people whose efforts need to be supported and recognized. For more information see justvision.com or theparentscircle.com.

Yasir Arafat lived for three years confined to his compound in Ramallah. He died on November 11, 2004. His death, like his life, remains shrouded in mystery. The cause of death was never determined, but there was a collective consensus from the medical community that he suffered from an unidentified rare blood disorder. A poll taken of Palestinians one month after his death revealed that 80 percent believed he was poisoned and the theory was supported by several senior Palestinian officials.

In a strange series of events, a dear friend's death may have been intertwined with Arafat's. Our friend Sami had taken a trip to Ramallah from Washington to visit his family. While there, Marwan took him to see Arafat and have dinner with him. After Sami returned to Washington, he collapsed and was taken to Johns Hopkins Hospital. It took almost eight months of tests at one of the most prestigious and advanced medical centers in the world for the cause of his collapse and abnormal blood tests to be determined. He had a very rare leukemia, almost impossible to detect and impossible to treat once it becomes active. Sami was convinced that he had been exposed to something while eating with Arafat. Sami went through a bone marrow transplant and other harrowing measures to save his life. He endured this for a year, until he died.

A few weeks later, I received a call from Sami's sister. She told me that Sami asked her on his deathbed to continue investigating his death. She said that while having dinner with Arafat in his Ramallah compound, Arafat had insisted Sami eat some of the food from his own plate. It was not uncommon for Arafat to scoop food off his plate and insist his guests eat it. Marwan had been there with several other men, but none of the other people who were present that evening had eaten Arafat's food. Sami was the only one. His doctors at Johns Hopkins believed he had been poisoned. They said that the form of leukemia he had suffered from was one of the rare types that could be inflicted through a virus. I passed the story on to some of Arafat's family members in the medical profession who had been present when he died. They too agreed with this theory, but until today no definitive cause of death has been declared.

Raymonda Tawil left the West Bank temporarily after the 2000 uprising, visiting her daughter, Diana, in Jordan and her son, Gabi, in the States. She published another book that was distributed in France, *Palestine, My Story,* which addressed the more recent years of her life and the plight of the Palestinians. In a phone call with Raymonda on March 27, 2007, in Tunis, where she was visiting her daughter, she told me that she had gone back to Ramallah so as not to abandon the struggle and found herself trapped, confined to her house. "My home became my prison again," she told me. She describes herself as suffering from post-traumatic and prisoner's syndrome. She has intrusive memories and emotional numbness and feels paralyzed. She has internalized the prison she lived in during these last years of seizure and finds it difficult to leave her house in Tunis. She recently sent me a moving letter that describes her situation well and recalls our days in Gaza:

My dearest Debbie,

I am delighted to receive your mail, believe me for weeks I do not leave the house in Tunis. I became a prisoner of myself since the siege of Ramallah, no matter where I am, I find it difficult to leave the house. The Prisoner Syndrome; that is what a doctor says about me. I got used to my jail; and going out of it needs more effort and incentives and struggle. I mean the physical struggle and the moral. During the siege in Ramallah, for over two years I was confined to one kilometer, I had no life at night except experiencing the fear of attack and the bombardment. In the morning you are happy to have survived the second day. I never forget when you told me to get out of that hell but I had left Paris after the Peace Signing to come to live in Gaza, Why? I wanted to live the experience, to live under the autonomous Palestinian Authority and belong to a country with a flag, an anthem and a passport. All my dreams have been in vain. Now in Tunis, this is the only Arab country with freedom for women. The woman here, according to the law, is an Empress. It is very different than what you saw. The Islamists have no ground in this country and even the President has forbidden the veil in official work and in public places.

Debbie, I always remember how you fought for your children. You reminded me of my mother, when they took her children from her. I had tears that I had hidden from you in our house in Gaza when Marwan did not want to let you see Tarik and Deena. I will never forget the image of Tarik holding you tightly and embracing you. Abu Hussein, who is now in jail by Hamas and was one of the main consultants in Arafat's office, told me he cried when he saw how you were prevented from taking Tarik and Deena. I feel so proud of your dynamism, your work and your contribution to human rights. I feel I am stuck. I could not achieve anymore what I wanted to do. I was stuck being the mother-in-law. Now I have to get liberated from this old imprisonment which I was involuntarily put in. I was suddenly without a name, I was only the mother-in-law. I was struggling to get my identity back. Now the situation has changed and I can be relatively free. I love you and Deena and Tarik.

Love Raymonda

I called Suha Arafat in Tunis on March 28, 2007, and asked her about her life since Arafat's death. She gave a little laugh and told me, uncharacteristically, that it may be better to remain silent. However, after a few minutes of conversation, Suha changed her mind. "I am sitting in Tunis with my daughter, thanks to the kindness and hospitality of the president and his wife, and I am watching Palestine deteriorate, I am watching our dreams disappear."

I asked her about the controversy that surrounds her regarding her knowledge about the millions in missing funds that Yasir Arafat was rumored to have diverted away from the Palestinian Authority into secret bank accounts. "This," she tells me, "is part of the propaganda" to destroy her, to destroy her husband's legacy. "You saw how I live, Debbie, a simple apartment. Why doesn't the media criticize queens who are buying millions of dollars of jewelry and luxurious items while people in their countries suffer? Is it because these leaders are puppets, so it is okay? My husband was a man for peace; he recognized Israel; he won the Nobel Peace

Prize. Those that didn't want peace won. The U.S. didn't help us, and the militants took over. When my husband was alive, the West said 'we have to wait for the next generation of Palestinians to make peace.' Now look, look in the eyes of our youth. The West has created the most violent, militant new generation. They only see blood. If they had not tried to take his power away and left him to lead, we would have had peace; things were hopeful, progressing. Of course we had little setbacks. Then we lost our partners for peace and now we have taken a thousand steps back. So, that's what I am doing, I am sitting back and watching how the West strengthened the militants, how they are creating another Taliban in my country. Things have happened that never happened before, books are being burned, journalists are kidnapped, schools are closing down, and people are divided. None of this happened under my husband. Yes, I am sitting here sadly as I watch everything we fought for, all the progress we made, die."

Fathi Arafat died of cancer two weeks after his brother, on December 1, 2004. Like Yasir Arafat, Fathi passed away while in a coma. He was never told of the death of his brother. Throughout his life, he never gave up on the belief that peace could prevail. He stayed focused on his positive vision, regardless of the circumstances—a lesson that was of the utmost importance to my own life. His Al Amal Center continues to live on and is supported by the Palestinian Red Crescent, although it has endured damage from shelling over the last several years.

Toujan al-Faisal was arrested in Jordan on March 16, 2002, and sentenced to nineteen months in prison. It wasn't the Islamic fundamentalists this time, but the Jordanian government. On

March 6, Toujan had published an open letter to King Abdullah II of Jordan on the Web site of the Houston, Texas–based *Arab Times.* In the letter, she accused Jordanian Prime Minister Ali Abu Ragheb of financial wrongdoing. The court convicted her on charges of "tarnishing the state of Jordan," defamation of the judiciary, "uttering words" before another deemed to be "detrimental to his religious feeling," "publishing and broadcasting false information abroad which could be detrimental to the state," and inciting "disturbances and killings."

Amnesty International rallied to support her, making the following statement on August 16, 2002: "This is a sad day for freedom of expression in Jordan. Toujan al-Faisal has been imprisoned solely for exercising her fundamental right to express her opinion. Sentencing Toujan al-Faisal has breached international human rights treaties which Jordan has ratified. . . . As we feared, the Jordanian courts are using new measures supposedly introduced to 'fight terrorism' to clamp down on the individual's exercise of the right to criticize government policy."

Toujan's lawyer reported that she was poorly treated in prison. Toujan went on a hunger strike, losing twelve pounds in a month. In addition, she suffered from cancer. On the twenty-ninth day of her hunger strike, she was released from prison by a special royal pardon. She told the BBC Online that she refused a wheelchair and wanted to walk out holding her daughter's arm: "I refused a wheelchair because I don't like the look, the attitude of weakness," she said. She wanted to run in the parliamentary elections of 2003, but the elections committee decided not to allow her to stand as a candidate. She filed a request before the Kingdom's Court in May 2003 but her request was turned down on the grounds that she had previously committed a nonpolitical offense.

✦ ✦ ✦

Shortly after our interviews, Queen Dina became ill and was diagnosed with Alzheimer's disease. I remember her memory lapses and her concerns over being tired and forgetful, and I feel fortunate that she allowed me to videotape her just before the onset of this disease. She is surrounded by those she loves and sheltered from the world in her beloved Egypt.

Baha Kikhia never found out what happened to her husband, Mansour. She is living in Dubai, selling her paintings and sculptures. She took her case to court in Egypt in 1999, claiming that the Interior Ministry of the Egyptian government did not adequately protect her husband at the time of his kidnapping. She first took her case to court in 1998, but it was dismissed on the grounds that she had failed to prove that she was married to Mansour and as a result had no right to sue. The court also said that it had found no evidence of error or negligence on the Interior Ministry's part. Baha then took the case to the Court of Appeals and won. She was granted 100,000 Egyptian pounds (approximately 17,000 U.S. dollars), the largest compensation ever awarded in a missing person case. In its ruling, the court said that the state is responsible for foreigners living in its territory. It noted that Mansour was a prominent international personality and "consequently, protecting him inside Egypt was a duty."

In 2001, my father was diagnosed with stage four liver cancer. I took him to many medical centers and specialists until a doctor at Georgetown prescribed an effective form of treatment. For the next four years, he took weekly trips to the hospital in Newport Beach and continued to make plans, researching ideas he had for a new company. He tried to solicit our support, which we gave in a limited manner, as we had all progressed in our own lives and no longer responded to his requests for all of our time and attention. He still had a great sense of humor, but I believe he experienced depression, not going out as he used to, not enjoying social dinners if he could not be at the helm as he had been before. He failed his driving test, for which we were grateful, but he continued to drive without telling us. He was caught and forced to wear an ankle monitor. The next day he took a taxi to a bike store and bought a moped. He crashed that afternoon, and two days after that, he broke his hip. A day after his surgery I went to visit him in the hospital and discovered he had checked himself out. I found him at home, in pain, and convinced him to let me admit him to a rehab center where he could have therapy and learn to walk comfortably. He ran away from every rehab center I found.

I finally moved him to a facility in Santa Monica. A few days later, he escaped through an emergency staircase, taking three hours to walk four blocks to Santa Monica Boulevard. The hospital search team found him hitch-hiking in his boxer shorts, trying to get home. The only things he had with him were ten dollars and a card trick.

His health deteriorated, not due to his cancer but because he refused the care he needed after his operation. He stopped eating and stopped going for his chemotherapy. He became weaker and weaker until he had no choice but to be admitted to a skilled nursing facility. His prognosis was not good. My brothers and I took turns visiting him every day. As he weakened further, unable to eat anymore, we were told he wouldn't live more than a week or two. The whole family came to California, and we stayed next to his hospital. We never told him the prognosis, but he knew.

One morning, the doctor told us he would probably not live until the next morning. My brothers were all in town, and so were the Yankees. They had tickets for the game that evening. My father and four brothers loved the Yankees. Yankee Stadium was their church, their place of worship. They knew the history of every player who had graced their bases since the beginning of the team. Only the magic of a Yankee game could prove to my brothers that there could be a higher power. And so it was on the night of October 6, 2005. As my father was slowly sinking into a coma and my brothers watched my father's labored breathing, they said to me, "We have to go to this game for Dad. He would want us there, and we know he will wait for us to come back." They got to the game just as it was starting. It was a playoff game against the Angels, and tension was high when Jorge Posada got up to bat in the fourth inning. He had the same first name as my father, the only Yankee ever named George. Posada took a swing at the ball, sending it high into the air. It hit a rail and continued to bounce from surface to surface until it headed back into the crowd, winding through the hundreds of hands that reached up to catch it until it landed right in the lap of one of my brothers. Thrilled, they called to tell me they had caught the ball for Dad and were bringing it right back to the hospital.

Shortly afterward, they entered his room and placed his fingers around the ball that Jorge (George) had hit to George. My father never let it go and died several hours later with the Yankee ball still in his hand.

I picked up my father's ashes about a month later. I walked into the office of the crematory after many phone calls requesting for me to come. "Who are you here to pick up?"

"George Jacobs," I replied.

"One moment, have a seat."

Not long after, someone walked out and handed me a small box. "Here he is," they said gently.

I put him in the trunk and drove to a café where I sat for a few hours before I felt up to driving home. I left him in the trunk for the next year. I couldn't think of a better place to keep him, and he'd always hated to stay still.

One day I mentioned to my mother, who had never quite forgiven him for ruining their marriage, that I had him in the trunk of my Mercedes.

"He always wanted to be buried in a Mercedes," she told me.

I was a bit confused. "Do you mean he wanted to be transported in a Mercedes hearse?"

"No," she said matter-of-factly. "He wanted his ashes to be put in a Mercedes and he wanted the whole Mercedes buried with him inside. I told him I wouldn't bury a whole Mercedes, but I'd drive around with his ashes in the glove compartment, and he agreed."

Even from the grave, my father had gotten his way.

Marwan Kanafani continued his role as senior adviser to and spokesman for Arafat and a member of the Palestinian parliament. In 2006, a year after Arafat's death, frustrated Palestinians voted out their current parliament and voted in Hamas, headed by Islamic extremists. Marwan's seat was lost. He went to Egypt, where he continues to live. He has just finished writing a book about his years with Arafat and the history of the Middle East. He is in constant contact with the children and sees them on their holidays. He is no longer married.

Deena Kanafani graduated in 2007 from Radford University in Virginia with a degree in political science. She shares her father's interest in history and politics and plans to go to law school, pursuing her interest in international law.

✦ ✦ ✦

Tarik Kanafani went back to the Middle East for his senior year in high school, studying at the American School in Amman. He returned to the United States for college and attended James Madison University in Virginia. He is now living in Los Angeles, pursuing his interest in the entertainment industry. He is writing two screenplays that depict the dilemmas of Palestinians and Israelis living in conflict.

When Deena graduated from high school and went off to college in Virginia, I decided to move to California. I worked with a friend's private equity company, running the entertainment division. I am currently living in New York and Los Angeles, and producing a theatrical film on the life of Queen Dina. I am continuing my work in conflict resolution between Palestinians and Israelis and have an organization dedicated to bringing Palestinian and Israeli screenwriters and filmmakers and musicians together to collaborate on projects, called Middle East Peace Through Art.

APPENDIX

PALESTINIAN AND ISRAELI ORGANIZATIONS WORKING FOR PEACE

Following is a list of Israeli and Palestinian organizations working in the field of peace building and nonviolence within Israel, the Occupied Palestinian Territories, or both. I encourage you to do further research, as there are many different kinds of activities and ways to support Israelis and Palestinians working for positive change. I have provided links only to Web sites with content available in English. The Just Vision Web site includes profiles of dozens of individuals working in many of the organizations listed below. Visit http://www.justvision.org/profile/ to read some of these in-depth interviews.

Adam Institute: http://www.adaminstitute.org.il/
Peace, democracy, civic education, and conflict resolution for Jewish and Palestinian citizens of Israel.

All for Peace Radio: http://www.allforpeace.org/
The first jointly run Palestinian-Israeli radio station. It produces news, feature, and music programs in Arabic, Hebrew, and English.

Alternative Information Center: http://www.alternativenews.org/
A joint Palestinian-Israeli political advocacy organization and source for information on the Israeli-Palestinian conflict.

Anarchists Against the Wall: http://www.awalls.org/
An Israeli organization that supports Palestinians' nonviolent struggle against the Separation Barrier.

Arab-Hebrew Theatre: http://www.arab-hebrew-theatre.org.il/
A theater and theater company based in Jaffa, Israel, that produces plays in Arabic and Hebrew.

Arava Institute for Environmental Studies:
http://www.arava.org/
An environmental education and research center at Kibbutz Ketura in Israel's Arava Desert. Students include Jordanians, Palestinians, Israelis, and North Americans.

Arik Institute for Reconciliation, Tolerance and Peace:
http://www.arikpeace.org/eng/
Works for reconciliation and tolerance; headed by the founder and former director of The Parents Circle–Bereaved Families Forum.

Artists Without Walls

A group of Israeli and Palestinian artists and musicians organizing joint exhibitions aimed at promoting understanding.

Bat Shalom: http://www.batshalom.org/

An Israeli feminist organization working for peace and social justice.

Behind the Wall: http://www.behindthewall.ps/

A Palestinian organization working mostly with youth to assess the consequences of the Separation Barrier for Palestinian communities.

Beit Arabiya Center for Peace

Salim and Arabiya Shawamreh's home in Anata in the Occupied Palestinian Territories. Their home has been demolished by the Israeli army multiple times and has become a symbol of nonviolent resistance. For more information, see http://icahd.org/eng/articles.asp?menu=6&submenu=5&story=32.

Bimkom: http://www.bimkom.org/

A group of urban planners and architects working toward "strengthening the connection between human rights and spatial planning." Their work focuses on Israel and East Jerusalem.

Bitter Lemons: http://www.bitterlemons.org/

A Web site that presents Israeli and Palestinian viewpoints, primarily on the Palestinian-Israeli conflict and peace process. It is coproduced and edited by a Palestinian and an Israeli.

Black Laundry: http://www.blacklaundry.org/

An Israeli group of lesbians, gays, bisexuals, transgenders, and others working for social justice and against the occupation.

Bridges Israeli-Palestinian Public Health Magazine:
http://www.bridgesmagazine.org/
> A jointly managed and edited Israeli-Palestinian magazine devoted to public health and peace issues.

B'Tselem: The Israeli Center for Human Rights in the Occupied Territories: http://www.btselem.org/
> An Israeli organization working to protect human rights and change Israeli policy in the Occupied Palestinian Territories.

Building Bridges for Peace: http://www.s-c-g.org/buildingbridges/
> A summer camp in the United States for Israeli, Palestinian, and American young women to learn leadership and communication skills and promote peace and women's empowerment. It also runs follow-up programs for Israeli and Palestinian participants at home.

Bustan: Sustainable Community Action for Land and People:
http://www.bustan.org/
> An environmental justice and sustainability organization focusing primarily on land and human rights issues in Israel's Negev desert.

Center for Jewish-Arab Economic Development:
http://www.cjaed.org.il/
> An Israeli organization run by Jewish and Arab businesspeople with the premise that "Jewish-Arab economic cooperation in Israel is essential for peace, prosperity and economic stability in Israel and the region at large."

Citizens' Accord Forum Between Jews and Arabs in Israel:
http://www.caf.org.il/
> An Israeli organization working to "bridge the gaps between

Israel's Jewish and Arab communities, and strive to implement systematic changes to improve the status of Israel's Arab citizens."

Coalition of Women for Peace: http://coalitionofwomen4peace.org/
An umbrella over nine Israeli women's organizations working for peace, equal rights for all Israeli citizens, an end to the occupation, and a Palestinian state.

Combatants for Peace: http://www.combatantsforpeace.org/
A group of Israeli and Palestinian former combatants working together to stop all forms of violence, end the occupation, and establish a Palestinian state.

Crossing Borders
A Palestinian-Israeli-Jordanian youth magazine published in English.

Economic Cooperation Foundation
An Israeli organization aimed at supporting Israeli-Palestinian cooperation in the political, economic, and civil society spheres.

Face to Face/Faith to Faith: http://www.s-c-g.org/facetoface/
A religious study, leadership, and peace-building program for Christian, Muslim, and Jewish teenagers from different conflict regions, including Israel and Palestine.

Faculty for Israeli-Palestinian Peace: http://www.ffipp.org/
A network of Palestinian, Israeli, and international faculty, with an affiliated international student network, working to end the occupation and create a just peace.

Folklore of the Other: http://www.folkloreoftheother.org.il/
An arts and education program aimed at promoting tolerance among the diverse communities in Israel.

EcoPeace/Friends of the Earth Middle East: http://www.foeme.org/
An environmental organization with offices in Amman, Bethlehem, and Tel Aviv that brings together Jordanian, Palestinian, and Israeli environmentalists to "protect our shared environmental heritage" and create the "necessary conditions for lasting peace in our region."

Gisha: http://www.gisha.org/
An Israeli legal organization working to protect Palestinians' freedom of movement.

Givat Haviva: http://www.giyathaviva.org.il/
An institute in Israel working to promote equality for all citizens in Israel and peace between Israel and surrounding Arab countries, including the Palestinians.

Gush Shalom: http://gush-shalom.org/
An Israeli peace movement calling for the creation of a Palestinian state.

Hand in Hand: http://www.handinhand12.org/
Runs three bilingual schools in Israel (in Jerusalem, the Galilee, and Wadi Ara) where Jewish and Palestinian citizens of Israel receive instruction in Arabic and Hebrew.

Hands of Peace: http://www.hands-of-peace.org/
A program that brings youth together in the United States in order to "foster long term peaceful coexistence among Jewish-Israelis, Arab-Israelis, and West Bank Palestinians by bringing

young people from the Middle East together with American teens in an interfaith setting."

Hashd: http://www.hashd.org/
The Palestinian office of the People's Campaign for Peace and Democracy, an organization that promotes a set of principles for Israeli-Palestinian peace.

Holy Land Trust: http://www.holylandtrust.org/
A Palestinian organization based in Bethlehem promoting non-violent resistance to the occupation and working on society building in Palestine.

Hope Flowers School: http://www.hope-flowers.org/
Teaching peace and democracy to students aged to thirteen in Bethlehem.

House of Hope International Peace Center
A center for peace in the north of Israel founded by a Palestinian citizen of Israel who is the author of several books on reconciliation and the traditional Palestinian dispute resolution method called *sulha.*

Interreligious Coordinating Council in Israel:
http://english.icci.org.il/
An umbrella organization over many interreligious organizations working with Israelis and Palestinians to "harness the teachings and values of the three monotheistic religions and transform religion into a source of reconciliation and coexistence."

Interfaith Encounter Association:
http://www.interfaithencounter.org/
An organization working to "promoting peace in the Middle East

through interfaith dialogue and cross-cultural study. We believe that, rather than being a cause of the problem, religion can and should be a source of the solution for conflicts that exist in the region and beyond."

International Peace and Cooperation Center: http://www.ipcc-jerusalem.org/

A Palestinian organization working to "develop proactive initiatives which support the social, cultural, political, and economic processes essential to a peaceful, democratic, and prosperous future for the Palestinian people."

International Women's Peace Service: http://www.iwps-pal.org/

An international women's organization working in the village of Hares in the Occupied Palestinian Territories to support nonviolent resistance to the occupation and Separation Barrier and to document and intervene in human rights abuses.

Interreligious Coordinating Council in Israel:
http://english.icci.org.il/

An umbrella organization over many interreligious organizations working with Israelis and Palestinians to "harness the teachings and values of the three monotheistic religions and transform religion into a source of reconciliation and coexistence."

Israel-Palestine Center for Research and Development:
http://www.ipcri.org/

A joint Palestinian-Israeli public policy think tank.

Israeli Committee Against House Demolitions:
http://www.icahd.org/

A group "originally established to oppose and resist Israeli demolition of Palestinian houses in the Occupied Territories." Its activities now include resistance to land expropriation, settlement expansion, bypass road construction, policies of "closure" and "separation," and the uprooting of Palestinian farmers' trees.

Israeli Palestinian Science Organization:
http://www.ipso-jerusalem.org/
> Promotes dialogue and interaction between Israeli and Palestinian scholars and scientists.

Ir Amim: http://www.ir-amim.org.il/eng/
> An Israeli legal organization that works for Palestinians' rights principally in and around Jerusalem.

Jerusalem Center for Women: http://www.j-c-w.org/
> A Palestinian organization for the advancement of women, peace, and human rights.

Jerusalem Intercultural Center
> Organizes activities and dialogue groups for residents of East and West Jerusalem.

Jerusalem Link: http://www.j-c-w.org/jl_principles.php/ and http://www.batshalom.org/jlink_principles.php/
> A joint venture of the Israeli organization Bat Shalom and the Palestinian organization the Jerusalem Center for Women, aimed at securing peace, a Palestinian state, and promoting women's participation in the peace process.

Jerusalem Peacemakers: http://www.jerusalempeacemakers.org/
> A network of Palestinian and Israeli interfaith peace builders.

Language Connections: http://www.languageconnections.org/
An online program whereby Israeli and Palestinian students make virtual connections through Web-based communication in English.

Machsom Watch: http://www.machsomwatch.org/
A group of Israeli women who observe Israeli military checkpoints to monitor human rights abuses.

Middle East Children's Association: http://www.mecaed.org/
A jointly run Israeli-Palestinian organization working to empower and support teachers to address issues related to the conflict with their students.

Middleway: http://www.middleway.org/
An organization whose activities focus around silent, meditative walks in Israeli and Palestinian areas with Israeli and Palestinian participants. The activities "combine spirituality with peace activism."

Mifkad: http://www.mifkad.org.il/
The Israeli office of the People's Campaign for Peace and Democracy, an organization that promotes a set of principles for Israeli-Palestinian peace.

Mosaica Communities: http://www.mosaic-coop.org/
A group working to establish integrated communities of Jews and Arabs in Israel.

Nablus Youth Federation: http://nablusyouth.com/
Working for youth, women and children's empowerment, creating connections between Palestinian and international youth, and Israeli-Palestinian dialogue.

Negev Institute for Strategies of Peace and Development:
http://www.nisped.org.il/
> Offers leadership training and support in the areas of small busi-
> nesses and organizations, conflict resolution, education, and
> democracy.

Neve Shalom/Wahat Al Salam: http://www.nswas.com/
> A mixed village in Israel, "jointly established by Jewish and
> Palestinian Arab citizens of Israel, that is engaged in educational
> work for peace, equality and understanding between the two peo-
> ples." Houses the School for Peace, a facilitation training program
> in Israel.

New Profile: http://www.newprofile.org/
> A movement to deemphasize the military in Israeli society and
> prioritize the civilian as opposed to the military profile of Israeli
> citizens.

NIR School of the Heart: http://www.nirschool.org/
> A program in which Israeli and Palestinian cardiology students
> study medicine together.

Olive Tree Movement: http://www.o-t-m.org/
> Provides humanitarian aid for Palestinians, including transporta-
> tion and translation for Palestinians needing treatment in Israeli
> hospitals.

One Voice: http://www.silentnolonger.org/
> A grassroots movement to involve Israelis and Palestinians as
> active participants in a peace process.

Open House in Ramle: http://www.openhouse.org.il/
> A center primarily dedicated to coexistence between the Jewish and Palestinian residents of Ramle in Israel.

Oz V'Shalom-Netivot Shalom: http://www.netivot-shalom.org.il/
> A religious, Zionist peace movement advocating the establishment of a Palestinian state and equal rights for Palestinian citizens of Israel.

Palestine-Israel Journal: http://www.pij.org/
> A quarterly publication produced by Israelis and Palestinians and focusing on issues related to the conflict and its resolution.

Palestinian Human Rights Monitoring Group:
http://www.phrmg.org/
> Documents human rights violations committed against Palestinians in the West Bank, Gaza Strip, and East Jerusalem, including those committed by both Israel and the Palestinian Authority.

Panorama: http://www.panoramacenter.org/
> A Palestinian organization based in Jerusalem working to strengthen Palestinian civil society.

Parents Circle–Families Forum:
http://www.theparentscircle.com/
> A joint organization of Israeli and Palestinian bereaved families working together for reconciliation and an end to violence.

Peace Child Israel: http://www.mideastweb.org/peacechild/
> Promotes coexistence for Israeli and Palestinian youth through theater and the arts.

Peace Now: http://www.peacenow.org.il/
An Israeli peace movement, promoting their political solutions for peace in the region.

Peace Research Institute in the Middle East:
http://www.vispo.com/PRIME/
Palestinian and Israeli educators and academics promoting peace building through research and education, and developing educational resources for teaching Israeli and Palestinian narratives.

People's Voice: http://www.mifkad.org.il/en/ and
http://www.hashd.org/
The joint Israeli-Palestinian grassroots peace initiative in which people on both sides of the conflict sign on to a statement of principles based on two states for two peoples.

Peres Center for Peace: http://www.peres-center.org/
An umbrella and support for many Israeli-Palestinian peace initiatives.

Physicians for Human Rights Israel: http://www.phr.org.il/
Works for human rights particularly relating to health issues in Israel and the Occupied Territories.

Public Committee Against Torture in Israel:
http://www.stoptorture.org.il/eng/
Monitors and raises awareness about the use of torture in interrogations in Israel and the Palestinian Authority.

Rabbis for Human Rights: http://www.rhr.israel.net/
An Israeli rabbinic organization "giving voice to the Jewish tradition of human rights" and working for human rights of all

Israeli citizens and for Palestinians in the Occupied Palestinian Territories.

Reut-Sedaka: http://www.bkluth.de/reut/COEXIST.html/
A Palestinian and Jewish youth movement within Israel.

Seeds of Peace: http://www.seedsofpeace.org/
A youth program based in the United States for teenagers from several conflict regions throughout the world, with follow-up programs for Israeli and Palestinian participants in their home areas.

Sulha Peace Project: http://www.sulha.com/
A gathering of Israelis and Palestinians to promote reconciliation, named for the traditional Palestinian dispute resolution ceremony of *sulha.*

Ta'ayush: http://www.taayush.org/
A joint organization of Arab and Jewish citizens of Israel working for equality for all Israeli citizens and with Palestinians in the Occupied Palestinian Territories to resist the occupation.

The Way
A Palestinian organization forming an umbrella over Palestinian nonviolence movements.

Windows: http://www.win-peace.org/
A joint Israeli-Palestinian youth organization with offices in Tel Aviv and Tulkarem.

Women in Black
A network of women protesting Israel's occupation of Palestinian Territories.

Yesh Din: http://www.yesh-din.org/
> An Israeli organization that opposes the violation of Palestinian human rights in the Occupied Palestinian Territories.

Young Israeli Forum for Cooperation: http://www.yifc.org/
> An empowerment program aimed at supporting young Israeli leaders who seek to "take an active role in shaping Israel's future and, specifically, its relations with its Palestinian and European neighbors."

Zochrot: http://www.nakbainhebrew.org/
> An Israeli group raising awareness about the Palestinian Nakba, or catastrophe, of 1948.

ACKNOWLEDGMENTS

I would like to thank the courageous women and peacemakers who let me tell their stories.

Special thanks to the team that helped structure this book and bring it to completion: my two editors at Simon & Schuster, Elizabeth Stein and Amber Qureshi; my agent, Gail Ross, for her belief in this project from the earliest stages; the creative guidance of Howard Yoon; and the editorial support of Kara Baskin and Edith Lewis.

And last, thanks to my sister Trinda Marks Steckler for coming up with our subtitle.

ABOUT THE AUTHOR

Deborah Kanafani has been director of international productions for the Palestinian Broadcasting Corporation, where she wrote and produced programs on children's and women's rights for the UNDP, UNICEF, and various European countries. She was executive director of Women in Film and Video in Washington, D.C., and a consultant for Oxygen Media. She serves on the boards of several Israeli/Palestinian peace organizations and is actively involved in conflict resolution programs. She currently lives in New York and Los Angeles, where she is producing a film on the life of Queen Dina.